The 8 Steps to SUCCESS

Simple Steps to Succeed in Business

Fourth Edition

Andy Albright

Scriptures taken from the Holy Bible:

New International Version®, NIV®.
Copyright © 1973, 1978, 1984 by Biblica, Inc.™
Used by permission of Zondervan.
All rights reserved worldwide.
www.zondervan.com

Designed by Kristin Marsh

ISBN: 978-0-9846501-7-0

Printed in the United States of America

Visit my website at AndyAlbright.com. Thank You!

To Jane Albright:

TO MY WIFE JANE WHO SHOWED ME THE TRUE
MEANING OF COURAGE AND DETERMINATION.
YOUR TRIUMPH OVER CANCER WHILE KEEPING
A POSITIVE MENTAL ATTITUDE IS A FEAT MOST
INDIVIDUALS COULD NEVER ACCOMPLISH. YOU
ARE MY ROCK, MY COMPASS, AND MY MOTIVATION
TO DO MORE.

Top 11 Managers (July 2013): Shawn Meaike, EVP; Alex
& Heather Fitzgerald, VP; Bill & Diane Lampe, VP; Stephen &
Hollie Davies, NM; Kyle & Beth Winebrenner, NM; Adam &
Beth Katz, RM; Chris & Cortney Long, RM; Patrick & Suzanne
Connors, RM; Paul & Tamara Roberts, RM; Mike & Noelle
Lewantowicz, RM; and Michael & Angie Owens, RM.

Mentors: Bruce Parker, John Roberts, Dr. J.L. Williams, Dr.
John Maxwell, John Phelps, John Haver, George Mohasci, Pastor
Mike Mitchner, Jim Henson, and Tim & Gaye Goad.

Colleagues: Jay Daugherty, Tony Hardee, David Hancock,
Marshall Pettigrew, Sandra Sheckells, Pamela Parrish, Preston
Sockwell, Missy Stipetich, Keith Hall, Chris Hill, Chris Reavis,
Katie Reavis, Robbie Craft, Mac Heffner, Justin Tripp, and Gina
Hawks.

John Maxwell

Ric Flair

"One of the reasons I'm excited about Andy is that I've watched him and I know him. I've watched him grow as a leader. And that DNA goes all the way down into his organization."

–John Maxwell
Christian Speaker &
Author of more than 50 books

"Andy wouldn't ask anything from you that he wouldn't do himself, and that's what makes people like Andy special. I'm beginning to think that Andy is the Vince McMahon of the insurance industry!"

–Ric Flair
16-Time WWE Heavyweight
Champion

Jon Gordon

Jack McKeon

"Decide to make a difference and success will find you. That's part of your new mission: You go out and make a difference and say how can I help people?"

–Jon Gordon
Best-selling Author

"One thing I've learned is that your attitude determines your altitude. Following Andy's eight easy steps will help you get started on the road to success."

–Jack McKeon
MLB World Series 2003 Winning
Manager

Bill Cowher

Lou Holtz

"I speak for only a few groups each year and NAA is one that I am proud to be associated with!"

–Bill Cowher
NFL Superbowl XL Winning
Coach, NC State Wolfpack
Linebacker

"I've talked with Andy and have read a lot about his company, and what he's done has really been tremendous. Congratulations on what you've accomplished!"

–Lou Holtz
College Football Hall of Famer,
Former NC State Wolfpack Coach

Burke Hedges

Clebe McClary

"With NAA, you have the company, the industry, the products, the opportunity and finally the support system."

–Burke Hedges
Author of Famous Book
"YOU, Inc."

"Thank you for what you do for young married couples today, who have a life, a future and a hope because of what you do. Thank you very much!"

–Clebe McClary
War Hero, Veteran, &
Founder of CMEA

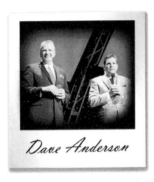

Dave Anderson

Randy Woodson

"Andy is the real deal and he's a lot like John Maxwell to me, There's this persona and they've done a lot of things and accomplished a lot but then when you get to know them they are the real deal."

–Dave Anderson
Famous Author &
Motivational Speaker

"N.C. State is proud of Andy Albright's accomplishments in building NAA into a thriving company that creates jobs and wealth for his employees, while providing a valuable service to those looking to insure their homes."

–Randy Woodson
NC State Chancellor

Chris Gardner

Josh Davis

"NAA® is becoming a distribution powerhouse. It has incredibly strong leadership, an outstanding sales team, and a highly successful lead generation program."

–Chris Gardner
Owner & CEO, Gardner Rich LLC

"You've been given a wonderful opportunity to provide for your family, to provide a great service for other people and you live in the greatest country in the world."

Josh Davis
5x Olympic Medalist, 3x Gold
Medalist

Andy Andrews

"I knew already that Andy was a dynamic leader. After meeting his family and talking to NAA, it was even more clear to me. I think that bodes well for anybody following Andy's leadership."

–Andy Andrews
Famous Author &
Motivational Speaker

Brian Tracy

"My friend Andy Albright has transformed himself to a multimillionaire from a "dollaraire" in just a few short years. Andy and his success have been an inspiration to me."

–Brian Tracy
Famous Author &
Motivational Speaker

Jane Albright

"Andy's experience and knowledge are a great combination of wisdom. His success comes from principles that are timeless. You will enjoy the way he communicates the journey."

–Jane Albright
University of Nevada
Women's Basketball Coach

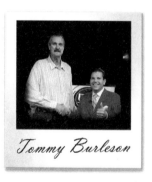

Tommy Burleson

"Andy is all about people helping people. That's what makes things go and makes things happen. He knows if you stay in your own little circle, there's no growth."

–Tommy Burleson
1974 NCSU Basketball Champion,
U.S. Olympian

Table of Contents

Foreword by Dr. J.L. Williams. . . . . *xi*

Profiles of Success . . . . *xv*

Introduction
Why Eight Steps? *21*

Chapter 1
Step One: Personal Use *39*

Chapter 2
Step Two: Work *49*

Chapter 3
Step Three: Listen *65*

Chapter 4
Step Four: Read *77*

Chapter 5
Step Five: Attend ALL Meetings *91*

Chapter 6
Step Six: Be Teachable *103*

Chapter 7
Step Seven: Be Accountable *115*

Chapter 8
Step Eight: Communicate with a
Positive Mental Attitude *125*

Conclusion
The Feeling of Success *139*
Resources *149*
NAA Agency Managers *151*

FOREWORD

BY:
DR. J.L. WILLIAMS

*T*his is not just a book about "How to Succeed in Business." It is a book about "How to Succeed in Life." That's because the same principles that will help a person succeed in business are the very same ones that will help them succeed in life. It is impossible to disconnect life and leadership. Success in one opens the door to success in the other. And it all goes back to attitude, as Andy emphasizes over and over again in this book. Since attitudes are the dress-rehearsal for actions, a positive mindset is absolutely essential for success in both life and leadership. So it is attitude more than aptitude that determines a person's altitude. Your mental attitude will largely determine whether you fly or flop in life!

Through the principles of this book, Andy rightly emphasizes business as ministry because that's why God created man in His image and likeness. As the Creator and Owner of everything (Ps. 24:1), God is the eternal Entrepreneur and ultimate Investment Capitalist. After creating man, He entered into a business partnership with the first man and woman and commissioned them to "rule over...subdue...have dominion... be a blessing," Gen. 1:26-28. God has not changed His business plan. He continues to entrust His resources to our stewardship. He expects us to maximize every opportunity for His glory and for the benefit of others. That's why the Bible teaches that our work and our worship are never to be separated. As Andy points out, our business is our platform to serve God and serve others. Simply put, other people are the purpose for our prosperity.

Dr. J.L. Williams
Founder of NDI & Mission Entrepreneur
Professor-at-Large
Carolina Evangelical Divinity School

PROFILES OF SUCCESS

"Over the last eight years that I have worked with Andy, I have seen countless individuals commit only to parts of his winning system, but none of them are successful. It is the individuals who apply all eight steps that climb to success. Andy's eight step program is the foundation of my success, and if you will commit to all eight, you will not fail."

"The 8 Steps to Success *changed my life. Today, I enjoy the financial freedom I always knew was in my future, and I attribute much of my success to* The 8 Steps to Success. *Andy's simple steps procedure directed my life, and it will take you where you want to go."*

Alex Fitzgerald
fitz@fitzgroup.com

"Reading The 8 Steps to Success *and actually associating with Andy has transformed my financial and family life. He has changed the way I see the world. And now by implementing eight steps and teaching to others, I am changing myself and everyone in my life!"*

Shawn Meaike
shawnmeaikenaa@gmail.com

"The eight steps were the catalyst for my personal transformation that started in January of 1993. Over my career, I have had the opportunity to be mentored by many great people in different industries, but Andy Albright's vision, endless supply of energy, and his The 8 Steps to Success *showed me how to achieve the ultimate success. It is the thrill of my life to be in business with Andy. Enjoy this book, and make your dreams come true."*

John Wilson
john@thejohnwilsongroup.com

"The 8 Steps to Success required me to focus on personal growth and self-development in ways I never did in the past. I now have control over my life instead of my life controlling me. I could never have stretched myself and my success without Andy's vision."

Stephen Davies
sdavies@thedaviesgroup.org

"When I first met Andy, my goal was to make a $100,000 per year. Andy said if I did the eight steps every week, and I did not make $100,000, he would pay me the difference. It sounded good to me, so I followed his eight steps every week. This is the point in my life when I started making over $100,000. He changed my life because his principles taught me self-improvement. Before Andy, I worked more hours, and I made less income. The 8 Steps to Success changed my thought process and gave me the knowledge to create more income."

Mark Womack
naawomack@aol.com

"The 8 Steps to Success has changed my life. My previous employers always seemed to center on the company's core values and the company's success. They never addressed the success of an individual the way Andy Albright does."

Andy Riddle
andy@theriddlegroup.com

"What Andy has done with The 8 Steps to Success is build a road map for success, and he's narrowed it down to eight areas. It really focuses on improving your life. It helps you increase your income, improves your relationships with your family, colleagues and God. It has a multi-faceted impact. It's got a simple, country-boy style. It's easy to read and it's simple to implement, but the benefits are priceless."

Alex Abuyuan
alex@alexabuyuan.com

"Andy has such an incredible vision. It's hard not to get caught up in it. He believes in you so much, how can you not believe in yourself? He serves you so much, how can you not give it back? If he's going to do that for me and my family, then I'm going to repay that in kind. He is so extremely loyal to his team that you just want to fight for him. You can't say that about a lot of people that they are willing to fight for you and that they are so loyal to you. That's what it comes down to. With his eight steps, he's helping people improve their lives and he's teaching people how to reach their dreams."

Adam Katz
katznaa@gmail.com

"The real measure of one's success in business is whether that success has been duplicated consistently throughout an individual's career. The 8 Steps to Success is a great guide and tool for leadership to constantly monitor and direct an organization. Andy's enthusiasm motivates an individual to set personal goals. His vision for greatness is contagious!"

Barry Clarkson
bclarkson@naaleads.com

"When I met Andy Albright my intended career path in baseball management ended and I headed down a different path. My goals, which were already big, got even bigger. We share a common belief about HARD work and we haven't let up since we started working together. I started following Andy's eight steps and I've never had as much fun working with people as I do now with Andy Albright. Thanks for all your guidance and leadership!"

Chris Reavis
creavis@naaleads.com

"No life ever grows great until it is focused, dedicated and disciplined. Moreover, I do not know any individual other than Andy that is so focused, dedicated to seeing individuals rise to the top, and certainly, disciplined in his leadership ability and in his reading and studying to take individuals to where they need to be. Good people do good things with money, and Andy is sharing his blessings with you through his The 8 Steps to Success."

Jane Albright
jalbright@naaleads.com

George Mohasci and Marie Osmond at a Childrens Miracle Network event

Shawn Bradley and Thurl Bailey

Mary Lou Retton

John Schneider "Bo Duke"

Miss America 2009 Katie Stam

INTRODUCTION

*T*his book is a guide for lifelong success, *yours!* While other people may want to limit you, I do not. Neither does God. As the Bible says, "if God is for us, who then can be against us?"

I would like to see you rise above the negative perceptions, feelings and influences that are holding you back. I want you to find the freedom in life that I have found and I want you to find a successful team where people are willing to help one another. If you are willing to come along, I am willing to give you step-by-step directions toward financial freedom and personal success—a complete program called *The 8 Steps to Success.*

I am not referring to being "comfortable" with a good income. I am referring to personal financial independence. Every day, my net worth grows because the people I have helped are seeing their own net worth grow, too. My most successful team members follow the program *The 8 Steps to Success* to the letter.

The 8 Steps to Success describes the actions that must be taken in order to experience success in business and in life. They are not "suggestions" to help you along. They are requirements, in my opinion, for anybody who wants to truly succeed. If you ask any successful businessman if he practices *The 8 Steps to Success*, he may tell you he has never heard of them, but if you ask him if he practices any one of the steps, he will certainly say "yes." In fact, these steps are likely at the core of what they do!

What follows is my personal story, the story of National Agents Alliance®, which is the company I helped start, and it includes the road map that can put you on the path to wealth and freedom. I suggest you read this book with an open mind, see the possibilities for yourself, and then decide whether you also have the desire to succeed and be financially free. Chances are, if you have purchased this book, the answer is yes. So, jump in and begin your personal journey to success!

MY STORY

I am a small-town boy from Union Ridge, a community in the town of Burlington, North Carolina, who has achieved financial and personal success through a company called National Agents Alliance® (NAA®). The company started with myself and two main partners in 2002. While building National Agents Alliance® into what it is today, my wife, partners, friends and I have been blessed to see a lot of other people become financially successful as well. In reality, my journey to success started way before my company started, so let's go back about forty years ago and start from there.

I was not born into a business environment or a wealthy family. I did not personally know anybody who was rich until I was an adult; however, I have always wanted to know how to be successful in the business world. Early on, I looked around and came to the understanding that some families knew how to create wealth while other families did not.

My parents were some of the hardest working folks God ever put on this earth. Their expectations in life were limited, though—so limited, that even as an 11 year-old boy, I sometimes felt that they did not know how good the "good life" could be. My father enjoyed working so much that he felt work itself was its own reward; he needed little else to satisfy him. My mother sometimes felt discriminated against, as if her life might have been much different, had she been given other people's resources. As far as I could see, my parents were just free to do as they pleased just like anybody else was, but they were unaware and did not understand how to create wealth, nor did they seem to understand wealth's true benefits.

I remember my Mama announced one time that we were going to buy a Cadillac. "A Cadillac!" she said! We were going to be just like the "big shots." What my mom brought home was a six-year-old blue monster, with a plush, lumpy back seat. She was very proud of this car and she had worked hard to get it. Despite (or maybe because of)the Cadillac, I knew that we had not achieved real "big shot" status. I knew, in fact, that we looked, at best, like "wannabes." Looking back, I'm still not sure my parents understood the difference between our Cadillac, the blue monster, and other Cadillacs that didn't have that blue monster appeal.

My parents did the best they could for us and were capable of great, low-cost inventions in making our childhood fun and memorable. My whole family loved baseball and going to ball games. My father converted an old, green Toyota truck into a camper with a cab made of pink and white aluminum siding and an actual trailer house door turned sideways for a back door. He constructed seats for the camper out of two by fours, and my friends and I sat on these makeshift benches on the way to the ball games. If it was 100 degrees outside, then it was 120 degrees in the camper!

I remember arriving at baseball games in that makeshift camper and seeing other families pour out of their air conditioned rides. We had our packed, brown paper sack lunches and they had their take-out restaurant food. These families often ate in restaurants, sometimes more than once a day! They ordered Coke and Pepsi instead of water with their meals. They read the menu from left to right instead of right to left. They lived in the grand homes our camper rolled by.

They appeared to know the secrets to wealth creation! As a kid, I sometimes wished I could have just gone up and knocked on the doors of the big homes we passed by and asked, "How did you do it? How's it done? What did you do to get all this? What's your secret?"

Now, do not misunderstand me. I had an incredible childhood with many fond memories. Although my family did not understand how to create wealth, they did encourage me to believe I could do anything I set my mind to. I was never taught that there were limits. Too many people have been limited by others from the start, and too many are limited by their own pessimism as to what they think they can achieve. I will always remember my Mama saying, "Andy can do anything he sets his mind to." I still believe that today!

Then there are those who believe everyone knows or should know how the world works, which involves finding a good paying job, saving, minimizing risk, and slowly making headway. These are the people climbing the corporate ladder, happy with an annual raise and some benefits, or selling real estate thinking they're successful at $100,000 a year because to them that's a lot of money. Many "succeed" in this way, but their view of the world and success is extremely limited. If that is what they want, I am all for that, but if they are complaining at that level, it is their own fault!

From the beginning, all I knew was that I needed to start working, so I did. In my farming community, I grew up working in tobacco, raking pine needles, and raising goats. I always tried to reinvest my wages in whatever business I engaged in, and I would try to increase its production capacity. I understood that more productivity equaled more money. This gave me one clue as to what was ahead, but not much more.

I have learned that success in this world is limitless to those who are willing to work for it, provided they don't limit themselves, and provided they don't settle, or just plain quit! Also, I know that God is in charge and rules all. I just know the opportunity is there to succeed!

LEARNING TO WORK

The people I knew growing up worked hard for a living, some improving their lives, but too many of them were just living to work and working to live. Some, like my father, were fortunate, he just simply liked to work. He had other interests and he found time for them, sure, but he never complained about working that I can remember. He never really desired to have more than he had, in this way, we were different. Still, he taught me the pleasures of hard work and how God has created us to work and to give back, for which I am truly grateful.

I quickly learned the rewards of work and dedicated myself to finding ways to increase those rewards, not only for myself, but also for others. I owe much of my success to the help and encouragement of others, and I do not want to leave this world without having paid that forward.

If I was not born optimistic, I became so at a time before I can even remember. I have learned the value of always projecting my positive outlook. My parents, I now see, encouraged that in me, with my dad always being happy in work and mama being a natural encourager and always full of joy. She used to tell people about me: "That boy doesn't start anything he doesn't finish." Hearing her say that made me believe in myself. I had this inherent quality of not giving up. NEVER!

You know the old question of seeing the glass half full or half empty? I do not see it either way. To me, the glass is always completely full. It is half full of water and half full of air, and air is a pretty important commodity. I have learned that success is built on obstacles, and that obstacles, even failures, are as important as successes. When selling, the misses are as important as the hits. Without some failures, there is no celebration in the successes.

Having confidence, optimism, and a love of work are helpful in getting ahead. As a young man, I saw that there are lots of people with those qualities and with plenty of ability, education, and even social positioning who never succeed financially. I did not want to be that way. I wanted unlimited opportunity, and I wanted to rise as high as I could.

While I always worked hard at whatever job I had, I was continuously looking, asking, and inquiring about how people were getting ahead. This natural curiosity led me down a career path that many would find implausible, if not slightly crazy. Few can probably say that since leaving the career for which they were educated, they have sold heavy equipment, raised goats for breeding and selling, hosted a radio program, and became an Amway "Sapphire" distributor, prior to finding their niche in life;

starting and running a multi-million dollar insurance marketing company.

I will tell you a little about how all this happened and you will get a feel for how I learned the principles behind *The 8 Steps to Success.*

I earned a Bachelor of Science in Textile Science from North Carolina State University in 1986. I chose to go to school there because N.C. State is an agricultural and mechanical school and both my parents loved N.C. State athletics. The Carolinas were rich in textile manufacturing in those days, and I knew that with a degree in textiles and my work ethic, I would be the kind of person companies would be looking for. I was somebody who could join their management team and help to build a company.

I met Jane Hooks my freshman year in college and we dated all through college. We were married six months after graduation. We wanted children as soon as possible because having them seemed practical, and then our lives together would be "set."

My senior year in college, I interviewed with every textile company that came to N.C. State looking for talent. I would sit down with a recruiter, listen to his questions, give him my answers, and when it was over, I would ask him (not worrying about getting the job at all) how my answers sounded. What did I say that impressed him positively or negatively? Most of the interviews I attended were just for the education or simply to practice interviewing skills. I knew I would get offers. I wanted to be prepared to interview well for the job I did want.

I was offered and accepted a position at Burlington Industries, whose personnel manager, Don Rose, I met playing golf. My first position paid $25,500 a year.

From the beginning, I dressed like management, like the people who had hired me, because I wanted to relate to them. I would do anything that was needed to succeed, that was my foundational attitude. My wife, Jane, was teaching school and our future looked bright.

However, I was soon dissatisfied working a job for a living. Even while I was moving up with the company, I was always aware that I was working for somebody else, and not for myself. I can remember one of my early bosses, a big Citadel graduate with a perpetual mean look on his face, Sherrill Taylor. I will never forget how he kept a toothpick in his mouth, which is how he kicked a smoking habit. I always knew I was in trouble when he switched that toothpick from one side of his mouth to the other and would say, "Albright, come here!" He never came to me. I always had to go to him. He would point out everything he saw that he did not like about my area of responsibility.

He was actually an incredible boss, and he taught me to look at operations with a critical eye. However, I knew after the first time he barked at me that I did not want my life to be controlled by somebody else. If I was going to succeed, I had to take control of my own life. I had to leave my J-O-B. I had to invest my money, my talents, and my ambitions into a profession that would allow me to grow my income and would also allow me financial independence.

FINDING AND FOLLOWING A SYSTEM

We reached a turning point in our lives through the most difficult challenge Jane and I have ever faced. In November of 1989, Jane began having health problems and was eventually diagnosed with Hodgkin's disease (a form of cancer) in January of 1990. We were still newlyweds at the time, having only been married for a little more than two years, and were certainly financially insecure.

I do not remember being scared so much as thinking, "What do we need to do to cure this?" I was planning, as Stephen Covey recommends, with the end in mind, and the end I envisioned was Jane being healthy again. That was all that mattered and I wanted to take the steps that would create this end. I also knew that ultimately, God was in control.

I was astonished by what the doctors told us. They said the success rate of putting Hodgkin's into remission was high, and that if you had to have cancer, this one was a good one to have because of the cure rate statistics. Great! Then, they told us that if we followed a strict program that would be laid out for us, her chances of getting well were increased dramatically.

I asked them, "So if we follow the prescribed steps, her chances of getting well are greater, and if we do not follow the rules, the outlook is worse?"

They said yes, that was it.

Now, we are talking about life and death, but apparently there are people out there who refuse to work a program that will save them and increase their chances dramatically. That made absolutely no sense to me then and still does not make sense to me today! Jane and I agreed then and there to follow the program exclusively and pray. In other words, we would pray like it depended on God, and work like it depended on us.

Jane's treatment involved a strict regimen of chemotherapy and radiology. It was a miserable but a necessary evil for her, with trip after trip to the hospital. I continued to work at my textile job, and Jane's mother and sister often went with her for her treatments.

Amazingly, through it all Jane kept working as a teacher. She would get treated, then work, get treated, then work. The pattern continued for roughly eight months. Our financial situation was such that she just was not going to quit working and see us lose what we had, which was not much! Jane's illness made us aware of how important prescribed steps can be and how few people actually follow a proven system, even when their lives are at stake.

Why would anyone not follow a plan for life over death!?

In my work life, I thought I was following a program that would lead to the unlimited success of which I dreamed. I was working the "corporate program" and asking: How can I get to the very top with my company? The president of Burlington Industries at the time was a man named George Henderson. I once saw a magazine article that said he was making approximately

$1.1 million a year. I still have the article. Someday, I wanted to be president of the company!

When I talked to people about my ambitions, they said it was impossible. The corporate system did not allow for people in my position to rise to the top. The mere possibility that I was going to be limited made me search for an alternative path. I was determined to achieve success on my own terms.

Also, Jane's serious illness made me realize I never again wanted to be in the position where both of us had to work. I was grateful for the courageous sacrifices my wife made, but I swore no one in my family would ever go through the same struggle again.

I began learning about franchises and multi-level marketing. I read everything about them I could. Both of these business models allow for increasing leverage through duplication of efforts. The more locations somebody owns, the better prices an owner can negotiate with suppliers. The more people that work for you distributing your products, the greater the profit you are able to collect from a percentage of sales. It sounded like the greatest idea I had ever heard!

Although I now realized that I needed to work for myself, I did not quit my job, and I continued to do well in my career. I eventually became an Area Manager. I directed eight supervisors, two secretaries, and 380 other staff. I received regular raises and was making "good money." I even joined the local country club! However, my earnings were limited, and they always would be.

In 1991, I was chatting with a colleague, Veronica Hedges. She was a successful Amway distributor. I asked her about the company, having studied it as part of my research into franchises and multi-level marketing. She had never spoken to me about it because of my position in the textile industry. She thought I would not be interested. However, I was very much interested, and I started learning the business immediately.

Amway is a great organization for making extra money, but I soon began to see that it was not what I wanted long term. It was hard to increase volume because there were so many competitors, and the products themselves had thin profit margins. I also learned something about myself while working with Amway. Initially, I found selling uncomfortable. Selling with Amway involves recruiting others to sell for you and building up your "downline." You are trying to convince either friends and family or complete strangers to come into your organization. That made me uneasy and uncomfortable, but I did it anyway and I became good at it!

I became comfortable selling Amway when I realized that the products and the recruiting were beneficial for the people to whom I was talking. Once I looked at it as helping them, I was more comfortable in the business. Actually, I began to "fall in love" with helping others get what they wanted in life!

I also learned the importance of buying your own product. You cannot sell others on something until you sell yourself on it. You have to counter your own objections before you can deal honestly with other people's misgivings.

Additionally, I learned the importance of numbers in marketing. If I only had five people interested, I had to have almost a 100 percent success rate to make any money. If I were meeting with 25 people, I only had to succeed 20 percent of the time. The more my contacts increased, the less pressure I felt. I applied this concept heavily when we started National Agents Alliance®. At NAA®, we work with qualified leads, generated by various ways of attracting interested people. The people we talk to have contacted us first, and they want to be called upon. Therefore, the discomfort I went through with selling Amway to friends and strangers makes what we do at NAA® seem like heaven!

While I was working full-time at Burlington Industries and building my Amway business at night, the company was telling us that the future of textiles was bright. All I had to do was read the newspaper to know the disheartening truth. The North American Free Trade Agreement (NAFTA) had just been passed, and textile manufacturing would be going overseas. I knew jobs were going to be cut, and I knew I did not want to work the sixty-hour weeks that would be required just to keep my position. Plants started closing—fast. I was praying for something else to do; something that I could take to unlimited heights.

Fortunately, Jane and I were now in a better position, financially and personally. With her cancer in remission, we had our life back on track, and we had our first child. This was 1994. We had developed our Amway income to where Jane could quit teaching school. I was bringing in around $40,000 a year after expenses from Amway sales, in addition to my salary at my textile job. Also, we had paid off all of our debt, except for our mortgage. Hooray! We were "back to broke." The pressure of Jane continuing to work was gone. Hooray again!

MAKING CHANGES

In 1997, I decided to quit my job. We decided to move back home to Union Ridge, my home. This is an area where Jane and I had both grown up, and it was where we wanted to raise our children. My parents had moved out of my childhood home, which Jane and I rented from them. We started working on it and making it our home. It needed a little work, but the land it sat on drew me back there. Dad always told me the land was not worth anything, but to me it was "home." A place to let the kids roam, a place to keep dogs and horses, and a place I saw as a paradise.

I did not have to worry about finding a job. I was going to focus solely on the continuation of building our Amway business. I became frustrated, though, by the limits of my Amway revenues. I thought the only way revenues could be improved was to find more than 24 hours to work in a day!

Jane and I were determined to find a business that would set us free financially and allow us unlimited opportunity. We would stay up late at night putting together ideas, writing out plans, deciding where we wanted to be in five or ten years. I had friends—including Adam Katz, Alex Fitzgerald, Stacy Boydston (McNeilly), and many others—that I talked with and dreamed with about what we would have one day and what we would be doing.

I got involved with a lot of crazy stuff in an effort to find what we wanted. I started a coupon business, a computer repair business, sold breeding goats, and traveled the country selling a line of heavy equipment, all while keeping up the Amway business. Eventually, I had thirteen unrelated businesses going at the same time! I was searching for something that would work.

Then one day, a cousin of mine told me, "Andy, anyone can make $75,000 to $100,000 a year selling insurance. I am doing it."

My cousin is a great guy and a great agent. This cousin, Russ Everett, I knew well, because his mom was my favorite aunt as a kid. I figured he could help me learn how to sell insurance. I was impressed that he was making that kind of money without an innovative, systematic approach. I thought if I applied what I already knew about marketing to insurance, I could do even better.

So, I began studying life insurance. I looked at the statistics. The baby-boom generation was terrifically deficient in owning life insurance. There were millions of people who needed it and did not have it, and there still are. I understood the need for life insurance, because of what Jane and I went through with her illness, and the importance of life insurance to anybody who has a family. There is a huge market out there, and it is something everyone should have. It is something they actually need if they care about their families. A good life insurance policy can save a family from poverty if something happens to the main breadwinner.

FINDING AN ANSWER

In July 2002, I met Philip Hudgins. Philip was a manager in a life insurance marketing business, and I joined the organization. During this time, his ideas about work, integrity and independence were a lot like mine. One day he said to me, "I bet you are thinking of starting your own company."

The idea for National Agents Alliance® began to take shape and was formed. I was thinking, "Might insurance be sold in an innovative way that would provide greater leverage?"

Two months later, a sharp, talented guy named Barry Clarkson joined forces with Philip and me. He brought his own experience and ideas to the table, and soon National Agents Alliance® (NAA®) was created and up and running full force. Barry and Philip each brought different talents with them that were desperately needed to start NAA®.

The idea was simple. We would take multi-tiered marketing into a proven business: selling mortgage protection insurance and life insurance. Also, we would do it right, by generating hot leads for our agents and by teaching them how to build their own futures. Helping others was critical for us to be successful. We would teach our friends to help people protect their families, and they would build a potentially unlimited income for themselves while doing so.

Our motto became: *"People don't care how much you know until they know how much you care."* We started applying that principle to ourselves with respect to our own agents.

As I write this, it has been eleven years since the origin of National Agents Alliance® which had its beginnings in my basement. We have grown to more than 10,000 agents, selling policies in all fifty states, and we are the biggest producing agency for some of the largest insurance companies worldwide. One of our goals is to achieve $1 billion in annual sales, and we are moving closer to that every year. NAA®'s plan is to own an insurance carrier and expand internationally.

I could not be a happier man. Jane has had no recurrence of her cancer. We have two wonderful children, Haleigh 19 and Spencer 16, who have grown up in the "paradise" Jane and I have made of my old home place. I have achieved the financial success I dreamed about as a small boy. We have so many friends and are blessed that they have enjoyed this ride with us.

God has answered many prayers, and I thank Him every day for what I have been allowed to achieve. I pray to be able to continue to help other people achieve success for a long time to come.

While I am happy, I am a long way from being satisfied. I will always be striving for a better future. Work is too much fun, for the company and our agents, and what we do at NAA® is too rewarding to stop now. I wake up glad to be alive, and I am raring to go! SHICKYBOOM!!

The company, National Agents Alliance®, and *The 8 Steps to Success* program can do the same for you. It can offer you the same as it has to me—riches—monetarily and emotionally—beyond compare.

It is a simple program, and easy to understand. However, you must stick to the basics. You MUST follow the Eight Steps.

"Let's get ready to rumble!"

–Michael Buffer,
Famous boxing ring
announcer.

At this point, that is just a brief summary of "my story", but it should be enough to get you in the ballpark of where we need to be. I am sure one day soon, I will give a much more thorough account of the whole story. For now, let's move to the major focus of this book—the 8 Team Player Steps.

Miss America 2008
Kirsten Haglund

Stakwell Yuenimo

Alex Abuyuan

Alex Fitzgerald

Shawn Meaike

CHAPTER 1

STEP ONE: PERSONAL USE

*T*he *8 Steps to Success* begins with integrity. If you plan to run a business that will set you free, your conscience must be clear! Trying to sell something you do not believe in is equivalent to stealing. You might make some sales and feel successful for a while, but you are going to be found out sooner or later. Besides, you are not going to be comfortable with what you are doing. Where is the freedom in that? There isn't any!

Integrity establishes a baseline and a firm foundation for everything you do. It is like having solid goals. If you have established goals, the decisions you make come naturally because they are oriented toward your goals. You often do not even have to make decisions because they are already made for you. You are just taking steps, one after another, to get to your goal. When you have integrity, you are committed to doing the right thing. The choices you need to make follow logically from this essential commitment to doing the right thing.

"If you want to ignite your business, ignite personally."

–Barry Clarkson

As a business owner, integrity begins with knowing, believing, and investing in the products and services you offer. How can you expect to represent something you do not own yourself? Also, how can you expect someone else to believe in your company if you do not believe in it? Being part of an organization requires participation. Participation means buying-in, literally, to the business. It means owning the product you are selling.

Why? First of all, you need to know the product you are selling. You can only do this effectively by selling the product to yourself. If the product is not good enough for you and your family, you are never going to be comfortable selling it to someone else.

You must decide which policy best suits your family's needs and buy it before you start selling. Don't tell yourself you will make some commissions first and then buy a policy. That is like a football player telling his coach he wants to play a few games before he decides whether or not he wants to bother learning the playbook!

Being a team member in your organization requires you to learn the playbook from the start. You should know the product you are representing. You should practice selling your company's products and services on yourself and with your family. After doing this, you will be able to gain credibility with your customers. Your belief in your product will show.

WHY FIGHT *YOU*?

You may get it in your head that you can wait until you start making money to buy your organization's products and services. Unfortunately, business does not work this way. Selling requires commitment. The very act of studying a product, learning enough about it to convince yourself that the product is a good one, should lead first to selling the product to yourself, and only then to selling the product to others. You can show commitment to your organization's products and services by buying them yourself. You can then convince others of its benefits.

Would you purchase an annuity or a life insurance policy from an agent who did not own a policy himself? Would you trust this agent? Would you trust the organization? Make your organization a part of your life, and then you will have no trouble convincing other individuals of its benefits.

I remember as a kid hearing that the Coca-Cola Company would fire any employee that it caught drinking another company's product. Any Coke employee that secretly preferred Pepsi and actually spent money on it, I thought ought to be fired. Whether it was true or not, it made sense to me, even as a young boy. I believed that if you worked for Coca-Cola, then by all means you should drink Coca-Cola. Being loyal to your own product indicates belief in that product. You should buy and use whatever product you sell, whether it is soft drinks, cars, vitamins, juice, or life insurance.

If you cannot bring yourself to buy your own product, you should be selling something else. If you cannot sell yourself on a product, how are you going to sell anybody else? You absolutely must find a product you can support wholeheartedly.

Are you a walking billboard for your product?

For instance, I am an N.C. State fan. I love the Wolfpack! When I was in high school, I made a decision to apply to N.C. State because I believed in the type of education the school had to offer. I knew that believing in and becoming totally loyal to N.C. State would help me find my niche and would also help me experience success. Now, N.C. State is a vital part of who I am. It is an integral part of my life. For that reason, I always feel comfortable praising the institution to others.

In the same way, I hope that you are sold on your college, on your business, on your product. I hope you believe in your product. When you believe in your product, you will find it feels natural to be a walking advertisement for it.

If you want to sleep well at night, you have to feel good about what you are doing in the daytime. I cannot live any other way and stay sane, and I doubt you could either. I like working with people who have integrity and enthusiasm about their "good." Who would not want peace through integrity rather than misery through dishonesty? A person with integrity and belief cannot sell a poor product (at least not for long), and a poor product will not find an honest salesman to keep it on the market for long.

Our product at National Agents Alliance® is life insurance. How successful do you think our people would be if they did not understand the value of owning life insurance? What if our people did not believe they were promoting a product that would pay off? How well would they sleep at night? What if our agents believed that life insurance was a bad deal, and that you are better off saving your money and investing in something else? If I believed that, the last thing I would do would be to buy a policy for myself. However, I know the value of a life insurance policy for anybody with a family. I know it is the surest and most economical way to ensure a family will be taken care of in the event something happens to the primary income earner.

When my wife was diagnosed with cancer, I received a quick lesson in the uncertainty of life. I was able to understand very clearly how tough life could be for a person who lost his or her partner, and how difficult it would be to provide for housing and children's education.

When we have sales meetings, I often ask our top producers to stand. Then, I ask all those present who own insurance policies (the product they sell) to stand. Without fail, the top producers all own policies. Many own multiple policies and annuity products.

Let us go a little deeper into why knowing, believing, and investing in your product is so important. **All sales begin with emotion**. People make up their minds based on their feelings, and then they back their decisions with logic. If you understand emotionally what it is like to buy your product, then you will see the logic in owning a policy to protect your family. Once your emotions are stirred and the logic of protecting families becomes clear, then you will catch fire as a salesperson!

Knowing, believing, and investing in your own product establishes a baseline of integrity and fulfills Step One.

By doing so, you will gather momentum for Step Two, Step Three… right up through Step Eight.

A Case In Point

Pam Moore is a top producer with NAA. The first thing she did is buy a policy on herself for the benefit of her granddaughter. As a matter of fact, the biggest reason she got started with us was thinking about her granddaughter and a medical condition that she has. It gets her very emotional.

Pam has went on to buy other policies for her family and to sell multiple insurance policies for her family and also several annuity products. Pam always stands up as a top producer. By selling to herself, she realized the benefits of these products have on her own family and she learned many other ways they can be of help to other families in different circumstances. She has become creative in finding ways to sell and promote the products to others as well as herself. By understanding the products through personal use, she can make sells in many ways she otherwise would not be able to make.

Mark Womack, another long time friend and NAA® agent, bought a policy for himself, and then he immediately turned to his father as his next customer. His father had never owned life insurance, and Mark knew his mother deserved the protection his father could provide with a policy. It took him a year and a half to convince his dad to buy a policy. Three years later his father suddenly passed away. Because this agent did not give up on making sure someone he loved was covered, his mother is now taken care of financially.

Do It Now

Great salespeople have a sense of urgency about what they do because they want their customers to enjoy the benefits of their products immediately. They are driven to succeed as soon as possible, because they realize there is no such thing as a "practice life." The life you are living now is the real thing, not a warm-up! Make the most of it now for both you and your customers.

Now, not later. No other way, no other time.

Sheikh Mohammed bin Rashid Al Maktoum, the ruler of Dubai, was asked if he was developing the Dubai Waterfront as a personal legacy or as a gift to his country. The development will extend Dubai's coastline 492 miles or 12 times its current length making it larger than Manhattan and twice the size of Hong

Kong. The sheik replied that he was doing it for the people of Dubai. It would create millions of dollars in revenue and provide opportunities for the people of Dubai.

When asked why he was in such a hurry to complete the project, he said that he wanted his people to enjoy it NOW. The opportunities would not be there for the people, until the project was complete. He wanted them to be able to reap the benefits immediately. "Now" is a key word to remember.

He did it for his people... NOW!

Mark's father waited a year and a half to buy a policy. He could have waited longer. What if he had? What if he had waited much longer? More to the point, the agent could have *let* him wait longer. If the agent had not believed in his product, he would not have been so persistent. If he had not sold a policy to himself, his father more than likely would not have purchased one either. Please, do not wait. You should reap the rewards today, not tomorrow.

We like to call Step One your first commitment, and it is really a commitment to yourself. After all, the best client in your life is yourself. If you can overcome your own objections, then you can overcome anybody's objections. However, if you start by listening to your own objections, and talk yourself out of owning your own products, you will become accustomed to talking others into not buying the product. You must make your business personal, and you must do it now.

Andy & Spencer

Albright Family
Atlantis 2008

Andy, Jane & Spencer

Bruce Parker & John Phelps
Fidelity & Guaranty Life

Dan & Shirley Neary
Chairman & CEO, MoO

CHAPTER 2

STEP TWO: WORK

Work requires putting forth effort, staying focused, and staying motivated to attain your goals. We have all looked through magazines dreaming of that fabulous vacation home or driving around in a sporty car. Motivation comes from wants and desires. Otherwise, we would be content to stay where we are in life. What an individual wants typically dictates his drive and motivation.

Opportunity is often overlooked because it's disguised as work

The *Robb Report* is a great publication if you want to see global luxury items. Be sure to check it out online at robbreport.com.

John Maxwell, best-selling author and leadership expert, states that an individual must overcome deficiencies or problems in order to attain motivation. How is this accomplished? You should gather momentum by taking whatever initial steps are possible. Then, you may formulate your plan of attack by clearly stating your objectives and compressing your focus.

Do you want that dream vacation home in 5 to 10 years? Do you want that sporty Jaguar in a year or in six months? How about just getting out of debt? Setting weekly goals rather than yearly goals will allow you to reach your destination in less time. Bear down to make the time go down. Only work will get you to your goals. Another favorite John Maxwell saying of mine is: "The **farthest** point between here and success is a shortcut." (Maxwell, 2009) Do not try to take shortcuts. WORK!

Bear down to make the time go down.

Work Smart

The first step in establishing a work routine is to make a commitment. Set a date and make it happen. Many individuals want to succeed, but they fail because they lack desire. Work is a physical or an intellectual effort directed to an end. Men and women are designed for work and, other than glorifying God, it is our main purpose. King Solomon, the wisest man to ever live, tells us:

"A man can do nothing better than to eat and drink and find satisfaction in his work. This, too, I see is from the hand of God." (Ecclesiastes 2:24, NIV).

You should not be afraid of work. Work is the constant in the achievement of every goal. The effectiveness of one's work and the amount of time it takes to reach the goal are the variables. Some people work and get things done, while others work and get very little done. It is important to understand the difference. One famous Amway speaker always says, "Trust only motion. Never trust only talk." (Greg Duncan, Amway Global)

Trust only motion.

You must decide what things you can do to become profitable. Once you have made up your mind, set out to accomplish a list of objectives. How do you accomplish this? What plan of attack will ensure these objectives will be met? How will you expend your efforts? Slowly and gradually over time, in repeated bursts, or grinding it out hour after hour? Your plan of attack will determine whether you have a balanced or unbalanced lifestyle. Having a balanced lifestyle, achieved over time, is the only way to have true freedom, no matter how much money you make.

Consider what would happen if you were to work 20 hours a day, seven days a week, at home. What an unhappy home life you would have! Your wife and family would be denied your time and attention, and they would be, more than likely, unhappy. Now, consider yourself working 20 hours a day but for three days a week, totally away from home. You will have a tendency to be more focused for those concentrated periods of time, lending yourself to be more productive and effective. This would still leave you plenty of time for family and other pursuits on the other days.

Bursts of concentrated effort are often the way to sell most efficiently. A successful sales agent may work only two or three days a week selling. These individuals are very organized and do something else with their lives the other days.

John Maxwell quoted his father as saying, "Figure out what you are good at and **DO THAT.**" People will call you unbalanced, and that is what you are. You ain't worth a crap at many things, so you need to be really good at what you are good at. In doing this, your life will only be unbalanced on the days that you are working hard, but more balanced in general.

You should learn how to work smarter and how to be productive. In building an organization, teaching individuals to work smarter is one key to being successful. Many people think they are working smart when actually they are busy doing nothing, or better yet, busy doing things that are non-productive.

My steps to success will not work if you do not.

Below are the four basic components of working effectively while building an organization:

- *Make a list.* The first thing you must do is to establish a list of contacts. Include first and last names with a telephone number. Specify how you know the individual. For example, are they a friend, a relative, or an acquaintance?

- *Prioritize your list.* Learn to prioritize individuals in establishing a call list. Which 10 people do you want to call first? Which 10 are you the most afraid to call? Which 10 people are the most successful? Find ways to categorize the list by dividing it into sections classified by the type of person.

- ***Call the people on the list.*** First, call the 10 people you are most hesitant about calling. Call them first to get them out of the way. You should start with your hardest sell and move backward. The crazy thing is you may recruit the great person that you thought would be the least interested.

- ***Keep records.*** Keep a list of the day and the time of every call. When you follow up, you can tell the prospective client that your call is regarding last Thursday afternoon's telephone conversation. Record keeping is critical. It provides accountability.

Work requires making a commitment, following the program, and adapting it to your plan of attack. During your intensive work periods, you should be methodical, and keep track of your activity. This requires monitoring your checklist in order to measure your performance.

Monitoring your performance is like having a doctor look at your temperature, blood pressure, height, and weight. By taking your vital signs, the doctor can evaluate your problem and help you. Otherwise, you may look healthy. Your vital signs help diagnose why you are sick and dying. In business, your "vitals" are your checklists and your records. They help determine if you are sick and dying or alive and thriving!

Like your medical patient file, your records must be maintained. They should be reviewed in order to be of any assistance. Reviewing your files allows you to grow. Your records are your proof that you have worked. Show me your calendar or your work records, and I can predict what your income will be in three to five years.

DIAGNOSE YOURSELF

One simple method of self-diagnosis is to keep a log of your activity. Set up a book that records your daily and weekly activity. Then, record your number of telephone calls, contacts, appointments, and sales. At the end of each day, look at your activity. At the end of each week, evaluate your work. At the end of each year, chart your growth.

I created a booklet called the *NAActivity*™ book for all National Agents Alliance® agents. It is the most effective, yet simplest way to measure your work, your effectiveness, and prediction of your future success. Every one of our agents use this book each month and they provide one to every agent they hire. Each new agent, in turn, provides one for a new agent that they hire. The best feature of the booklet is that all proceeds go to a charity called Children's Miracle Network. The following is an example of a weekly activity log for a sales agent:

Activity Log	Telephone Calls	Contacts	Appointments	Sales
Monday				
Tuesday				
Wednesday				
Thursday				
Friday				
Saturday				
Sunday				

Any successful, growing, profitable agent in your organization can diagnose and prescribe action based on this simple chart:

- Few Calls = Poor work habits or small dreams

- Good number of calls + Few appointments = Poor phone skills or lack of urgency

- Good number of appointments + Few sales = Poor in-person closing skills or lack of urgency

- High calls + High appointments + High sales = $$$ + Dreams Come True!

Whether your profession is in sales or another line of business, the principles are the same. You should monitor and control your work habits. Monitoring your own work habits keeps you accountable to yourself. (Agents: Monitor your daily activity with the *NAActivity*™ book available at <u>ShopAtNaa.com</u>.)

Business is very much like dialing the combination to a safe. You must turn the dial in a specific direction and stop on a specific number in order for the safe to open. Only the correct combination will unlock the safe's rewards. By focusing your work schedule on aspects you can control, such as having the correct combination and working more efficiently, ultimately you will become more effective.

If you are not working effectively, change what you are doing! When I used to fish with my dad, there would be times when the fish were not biting. Dad would tell me, "You're not holding your mouth right." His point was that he did not care what I changed about what I was doing, it just was not working, and I needed to change SOMETHING!

You must understand that if what you are doing is not working, "you must be holding your mouth wrong." Change something! Our top coaches and leaders can listen to an ineffective call and diagnose all kinds of errors that need to be corrected. If people are not answering your calls, change the time of day you are making the call, change the day of the week, whatever…but change something!

LINE UP TO FIRE UP

Some people are very organized. Their files are neatly color-coded and alphabetically organized. This is great, but it does not pay the bills. In business, you are paid on what is done and what goes out the door. This is why it is important to focus your efforts on items you can control, such as your attitude, your work ethic, and your character. Then, get out there and go to work!

DOGS IN THE HUNT

One of my favorite memories as a boy was hunting with my dad. He raised beagles for rabbit hunting. He never talked about how his dogs hunted for pleasure. What he talked about was how they loved to work. All rabbit hunters and bird hunters use that same terminology when talking about their dogs. They all say they love to "watch them work."

The most pleasurable part of the quail hunting experience is the bird dogs, who are trained to locate and retrieve the quail. The pleasure is not so much in hunting the birds as it is in watching the bird dogs "work." A well-trained dog, bred with the keen instincts of finding, pointing and retrieving birds, is a beautiful thing to watch. They are single-minded. FOCUSED. It is what they were born to do, what they are trained to do, and what they do well.

When hunting dogs are turned loose, briar bushes do not bother them, the heat does not bother them, the cold does not bother them. They are just focused on the hunt, focused on their work. Their work is, in fact, their reward. I have heard old men out in the field say many times: "Man, I love to watch them work." Then their next words always seem to be, "You can tell how much they enjoy it."

A favorite saying of mine is, "A dog in the hunt ain't got no fleas." When a bird or rabbit dog works, he is aware of nothing else. The same dog, in his kennel, if he has fleas, will let them bother him. He will sit and scratch. However, that same flea-ridden dog does not know fleas exist when he is on the hunt. He is that focused.

Find work you can put yourself into—work you can enjoy. Then, focus and achieve. Being hard at work can focus your mind, similar to when you are frightened. If you are threatened and scared, you can accomplish anything because of the adrenaline. When in danger, you are so focused nothing exists except getting to safety. If your life is at stake, you will run through a plate glass window, jump from a tall building, anything, without giving it a

He ain't got fleas. thought. Focused work can have a similar effect. Focused work is exciting, like adrenaline-pumping fear. Like adrenaline, work can set your spirit free. A man in touch with the work he was designed to do, is like **a dog in the hunt**. He can accomplish his goals, he enjoys doing it, and does not realize he has fleas.

GET UP IN THERE

Dad always used to tell me: "You've got to get up in there." I would be playing Little League baseball, and my mind would not be on the game, or I would be fearful or shy about being at bat.

Get up in there man! He would yell to me, "Get up in there, boy!" It is the same way he would talk to Molly, his beagle, if she was nervous about going into the briar patch after a rabbit. "GET UP IN THERE!" It's something I now say to an agent who is nervous about making calls or closing deals.

HAVE A GOAL

Here is one last thing my father would say that is helpful to remember: "When you are standing around is when you will get into trouble." To me, that means when you are not working toward a goal, you have a tendency to procrastinate, be lazy, become complacent, and, in other words, "get into trouble." A lot of times, when you are not working toward a goal, it is because of fear.

There is a certain fear in selling. There is a fear of rejection or of losing a sale when you badly need money. There is a fear of not being liked or of insulting someone. Those fears have to be put aside in order to get started, to make a phone call, or to ask for the sale.

We have sales agents who are doctors, college professors, and attorneys. I will talk to them the same way as I do any other agent in our organization. I will tell them to "get up in there." I will even put a phone receiver in their hand and tell them to "do this with the other hand," and I will make the motion of dialing the phone. Sometimes getting people to work is a sales job in itself!

Work is an outward sign of your faith. Most people have some spiritual beliefs, and I often ask them, "Do you have faith in your religion? If you do, you act on it, don't you? In the same way, do you believe that dialing numbers will get you appointments?"

They will tell me, "Well yeah, I do, but..."

This brings up my billy goat saying. "Don't butt me!" The word "but" really bothers me. Do you have faith or do you not? Should you make your calls? If the answer is yes, then do not "but" me. People all too often allow their "butts" to get in the way of their success. In other words, get off of it and do something!

Another question to ask is: "Are some results, any results, better than no results?"

Well, what about bad results, you might ask.

What bad can result from making a call, from making an effort? Well, you could offend someone and not get a sale. However, not making that call guarantees you will not make that sale!

Sometimes I will tell people to make a certain number of calls just to help me out with reaching a goal of number of calls made. My purpose is to get them started. People love to help others out, and it can be easier for them to start off by thinking they are helping out, which they are! If they believe what they are doing is helping me and helping the team, they will do it. In the same way, they will overcome a fear of selling once they believe that owning life insurance helps people.

Then, I'll say: "Please, don't even worry about having good results."

I simply want them to engage in the activity without worrying about the results. Just get started. Dial the phone! With enough activity, a salesperson will get a certain number of appointments. Once an appointment is set, that salesperson will follow through because going to the appointment is a lot easier than getting the appointment.

Hard Work Made Easy

I believe in working hard to make work easy. Making a hundred calls to get 10 appointments is the hard part. Once you have done the hard part, going to the appointments is easy! Once at the appointment, making the sale is even easier if you believe in what you are selling and if you know the person you're selling to will benefit from the purchase. It's all work, but it doesn't all have to be hard.

Work produces results, which is why the work itself is important. Work can also produce effectiveness if you are consistent and learn from your efforts. Work, therefore, can be its own reward.

When I was a kid, my father always seemed to have me cutting and splitting firewood, not one of my favorite things. There's an old saying, though, that chopping firewood warms you twice. Even if someone were to steal your firewood, you would have already warmed yourself up chopping! So work itself is a reward.

Lack of clarity leads to lack of activity. That's why I don't like to give people three different things to do. No matter who you are, I try to ask you to do only one thing at a time. Some people are impatient and want to know, "What will I do next?" and I will tell them to just wait until they have done the one thing first. Sometimes they get angry because they think I doubt that they are capable of doing more than one thing. So they do the one thing as a challenge to get me to tell them what to do next. It creates an emotion, and emotion creates activity.

You see, I have a crazy faith that activity produces results, because I remember starting out on day one, upside-down, naked and screaming, trying to sell the doctor on the fact that I could breathe and that he could quit beating my bottom, which worked. Sometimes we're selling and don't even realize it.

But Work Takes Practice

Work that produces results must become routine. The more practiced you become at something, the better you get at it.

When we played basketball as kids on our old concrete court at home, we put together a victorious play book by using the same strategic, game-winning play over and over. We developed a play that worked and we would concentrate on that play until we could just crush opposing teams with it. Our goal was never to be entertaining; our goal was to get results. We were never ashamed to run the same play over and over. We were not "hope for a good game" people. We were "hope to win" people. Staying with what we found that worked, and learning to perfect it, brought the results we were ultimately after: wins. Then we could laugh it up and entertain ourselves afterward.

I started out—upside down and naked!

So, I am talking about using a certain formula with the work, just as my 8 Steps is a formula. I am trying to get you to experience successful work habits without having to learn them for yourself. Like I tell people, you do not have to jump off a building to find out it is going to hurt. Likewise, you do not have to go out and try a thousand ways of working to find a way that gets results. You do not have to believe everything I am telling you in this book, but I am telling you, it is a proven fact. Just **act like** you believe it and do it. After you see it working, then you will believe it! Doing what I am teaching produces activity, and activity produces what? It produces results. That's right!

Commitment to continuity builds mental stability. What I mean by this is, if you are trying to stay mentally focused in whatever you are doing, remain consistently active. If you are consistent in your work habits, you will create mental work stability. As Vince Lombardi once said, "The harder we work, the harder it is for us to surrender."

Just like our pickup, playground-playing basketball team, the harder you work, the better you get. Going easy does not make for good results, but once you have established effective work habits, working does not have to be hard. Through consistent work you can learn to have an effective work level in a short period of time.

WORK EFFECTIVELY AND STAY BALANCED

The guy I mentioned earlier, Mark Womack, is a man in our organization who has found his effective work level. He began in the insurance industry by working very hard, and he learned to work very effectively. He was licensed in about six days, and he worked really hard to create a six-figure income. Once he had his methods polished, he was able to lessen the number of days he worked in a week, and he still maintained his income. He watched more television than any man I have ever known, but he was consistent in his work habits. When he worked, he worked, and he worked every week using consistent methods that yielded results.

You need to be balanced. Some people put in 80-hour work weeks. I have no problem with that if that is what you need to do to get where you want to be. My point is, though, that while you are working your 80 hours, you need to be learning to work effectively. Then, if you have learned to work effectively, you should be able to cut back. You have to have the kind of balanced life I talked about earlier to have any freedom. You need time for family, hobbies, travel, personal development, and basic living. Life is FOR living!

Commitment to continuity builds mental stability.

Sometimes an effective worker can change patterns and move to a higher level. Mark Womack worked a two or three day work week and watched television for six years. Then one day, he was in my office reading his personal biography that hung on the wall of our office with his picture, and he started crying. He realized how much my team and I had helped him with his success, and realized he had not done the same for anybody else. That very day he started working a different program, and for the last two years he has led the most consistently growing NAA® team in the United States, helping hundreds of others achieve their goals. He has been steady in building his team and helping others.

You see, Mark has set a higher goal for himself. He is now working five or six days a week because he wants to, and he gives heavily to charities he believes in, because he wants to give back. His higher level of commitment has given him that ability and that reward.

Don't Just Sit Around

I will end this section with a story. You may have heard of Larry Walters from back in the summer of 1982. Larry, a 33 year-old Los Angeles man, bought 45 helium balloons from a local Army-Navy surplus store. He secured himself to a lawn chair, loaded up a six-pack of beer, a camera, and a pellet gun, which he planned to use to pop a few balloons when it was time to descend. Then he hopped on board.

His plan was to float about 30 feet above his back yard and come down in a few hours. He ended up floating at an altitude of over 11,000 feet, into LAX airspace. (An incoming airline pilot radioed the tower and described seeing a man in a lawn chair.) After 14 hours in the air, Larry came back down. When asked why he did it, he stated that **a man could not just sit around**. (Mikkelson, 2005) (Television show Urban Legends Verified)

Successful workers are like Mark Womack, Larry Walters, and my daddy's bird dogs. They cannot just sit around and wait for success to come to them. They have to just "get up in there!" They have to go out and work to find it. They get pleasure in their work and find thrills in attaining their goals.

Excitement, conviction, and execution are the name of the game. By putting forth effort, they see results.

There's a difference between simple and easy. Simple means it's NOT COMPLICATED. Easy means it requires no effort. These steps, like me, are simple.

Donnie Osmond &
George Mohasci

Andy & Alex Fitzgerald
Bahamas

Jason & Tawny Carey

Jeff Schmid
President of M.O. Bank

John Roberts

CHAPTER 3

STEP THREE: LISTEN

Many ideas are communicated only when the listener pays attention to more than just the words that are spoken. Good communication is achieved only when people use their eyes, their ears, and their minds. Good communication requires us to become active listeners.

Successful individuals are active listeners. They listen to what their partners are telling them, they listen to what customers are saying, and they pay attention to what other successful people are doing. They are successful because they stay actively involved. They absorb information both through the words they hear and the speaker's body language.

> "God gave man two ears but only one mouth that he might hear twice as much as he speaks."
>
> –Epictetus
> Greek Philosopher

LISTEN TO LEARN

Active listening is an important key to knowing your customer, and good listening skills usually have to be cultivated. Even very intelligent people often have poor listening skills by nature. Being a good listener is a rare aptitude, but with a little practice can be learned by anyone. Our culture with all of its noise inhibits listening, which makes the practice of active listening all the more important. If you have kids, just try walking through the room when they are watching television. They will not even know you are there! You have to stand in front of them to get their attention.

So how do we learn to listen in a business context?

"Listen" is a verb. It indicates activity and action. So, now you ask: "What action is involved in listening? There is no action. My ears just automatically operate!"

Not true! Listening requires mental and sometimes physical activity.

For example, imagine that I am talking to you. Are you taking notes? When you take notes, you both hear and see. You are listening to the words I am saying with your eyes, as well as with your ears. Are you looking at me? That is very important! Listening occurs with your eyes, also. Studies have shown how much meaningful information is conveyed through body language.

When we talk about being a good listener, we are also talking about being a good communicator as well, because when you listen, you should be translating for yourself the meaning of what you are hearing by putting it into your own words. You have to actively engage in what is being communicated to know what you are really being told.

Suppose a potential customer is talking to you. Is the look on his face in agreement with his words, or does his or her facial expression tell a different story? Be sure you know, or you may miss the truth. If you miss the truth, you will miss the sale.

LISTEN TO UNDERSTAND

The Book of Proverbs in the Bible has so much wisdom in it. I call it a book within "THE BOOK." To me, the Proverb of Proverbs is this: "Seek first to understand."

In understanding people, for example your customers, you have to put aside your own ego, your wants, and your desires. If you walk into someone's house worrying about making a sale, you are working out of fear. However, if you forget your fears and go into a home with a true desire to help, your empathy level increases, your interest level increases, and you listen and learn. If you go into someone's home and lead with your heart, and you really care about the person you are meeting, then the fear will evaporate. You are now trying to understand the way the other person thinks, rather than trying to change the way he thinks. Your customer gets to stay within his comfort zone and does not feel challenged. A comfortable customer often pursues the sale.

Listening is an art that must be learned. It takes time and concentration. Some of us are better at it than others. Learn to listen to your mentors and your customers because they have a wealth of knowledge that is constructive and free. Furthermore, doing so sends the message that you are eager to learn, and that you are looking for any advice they can pass your way. It shows your customers that you have a genuine concern for their welfare. Below are a few simple rules to follow when listening:

- *Do not interrupt:* Allow the speaker to convey his thoughts without rushing to convey your thoughts and ideas. This shows respect and genuine interest.

- *Sit Down:* If the situation presents itself, sit directly in front of the speaker. This lets the speaker know he has your full attention and that you are committed to what he has to say.

- *Maintain Eye Contact:* Directly face the speaker. Keep your mind open to receive the information. Maintain eye contact and occasionally nod your head to let the speaker know you comprehend what he is saying. If you are in a meeting or a conference, it may be impossible to maintain eye contact. In these situations, it is OK to take notes to reinforce key information, and to show you are paying attention.

- *Acknowledge His Words:* An occasional head nod shows the speaker that you are actively engaged in what he is saying. Periodically say, "Yes," "By all means," "That is very true," or "I understand."

- ***End with Open Questions:*** When the speaker has completed his thoughts, end the discussion with a couple of open questions. Open questions require more than a "Yes" or "No" answer. For example, rather than say, "That must have cost you a sale, you might say, "Why do you think you lost the sale?" Then follow up with, "What do you plan to do on your next sales call to make sure this does not happen again?"

One thing I have found to be very effective is to mimic people mentally or duplicate the facial expressions of the person speaking. I turn what the person is saying into a performance, a dramatic role, that I am learning to play. When I do this, I can not only repeat what the person has said, I can even duplicate the facial expressions he used while saying it. I have found time and again this helps me really understand what the person wants me to know.

While you cannot always do this with private conversations, tape record whenever you can. This takes some forethought on your part, which shows commitment to active listening. Showing up at a seminar and bringing a tape recorder with you means you thought beforehand about actively listening to what was going to be said.

LEARN THE VALUE OF MEETINGS AND SEMINARS

I am a believer in learning through reading. The wisdom in books is there for anybody who will read. (I'll talk about that in my next chapter). I also believe in attending seminars for the same reason.

Find speakers whose outlook you appreciate, and get yourself in front of them by attending their seminars and workshops. Like books, seminars are a great way to pick up valuable information, and there is no better place to practice active listening. Seminars also provide a learning experience you cannot get with books.

Many times I have had the experience of reading a mentor's book and then listening to him or her deliver a seminar on the same subject, and I have picked up things I had completely overlooked when reading the book. Being face to face, on the front row, is priceless.

Also, a book's words are fixed in place, but when the author is speaking on the same topic, he is likely to make some off-the-cuff remarks. As he is talking, things are going to come into the author's head that he will realize are worth saying, and he will say them. When he **Be on the** speaks, he is giving you a revised edition of **front row!** the book.

While some seminars are free, some can cost a lot of money. I do not mind spending money on a good seminar, because I do not mind paying for a good education. If I am paying good money for a seminar, I want to get ALL I can from it. That is why I recommend tape-recording and taking great notes as active listening tools whenever possible.

Let us say you have paid a lot of money to attend an exclusive seminar, as much as $5,000. Are you going to attend without a tape recorder? You are willing to pay $5,000 to hear something said one time when for that price you can take the seminar home with you and hear it again and again by simply taping the seminar?

Sitting through even excellent seminars can sometimes be trying. Your focus naturally goes in and out, like a yo-yo moving constantly up and down. You are hearing what is said and then you are not—your mind has wandered. You are going to miss things, no matter how dynamic the speaker is. Remember, it's not the speaker's job to be a good speaker as much as it is your job to be a good listener. Getting the speaker's message on tape lets you review it for what you might have missed. Do not let the fact that you are recording be an excuse for not paying active attention while you are there.

How do you overcome losing focus? You have to keep your mind alert. You have to watch the speaker closely, like I have said. You have to listen actively, asking yourself what the speaker means to try to get into his mind as much as possible. Even all this activity can cause you to miss things. Listening to a public speaker is not like having a one-on-one conversation where you can interact and get clarification on the spot, which is why tape recording is important.

As President and CEO of National Agents Alliance®, I attend seminars all over the country. When I do, I always sit in the front row, or as close as I can get. Being up front keeps me focused. I preach this to the members of my organization to the point where we have actually had some scuffles at seminars with all of us trying to get a seat in the front row! Setting that "up-front" mentality in your organization, you attract people who want to listen, who want to be active listeners and learners.

Promote an 'up-front' mentality.

If up-front seats are more expensive, I pay the extra cost. It is the same as going to a baseball game and paying for seats behind the dugout as opposed to cheap seats in the left field bleachers. If the seminar is free, well, why would I not take full advantage by sitting up front anyway to get as much out of my time as I can?

Sitting up front, like bringing a tape recorder, means you are making a commitment to benefit as much from the speaker as you can. Being physically close to the speaker lets you pick up on facial expressions and gestures you might otherwise miss.

When you are in a private conversation, you cannot just mimic someone's facial expressions in front of them, except in your own mind. However, being in the front row at a seminar, you can. I recommend it. I even recommend exaggerating the speaker's facial expressions to stay more attuned with what he is saying. I have noticed that if the speaker sees you so attuned that you are imitating him, he actually takes off on this and becomes even more animated, feeding off of your interest. He sees you going along with him, so he sells it even harder and you get a higher-level message from him!

Recording conversations in an interview can serve another

purpose. When I am talking one-on-one with someone important, I can be nervous. I can be thinking about my next question while he is answering the last one. I can be excited about being in front of this person and miss some of what he is telling me. No matter how thoroughly I have trained myself to be a good listener; emotion, excitement, and nervousness can diminish my capacity to listen. You cannot always stop someone to get clarification, either. Likely, you will not know you have missed something until it is too late. Recording the conversation lets you sit down later and hear clearly what was said.

Finally, a recorded speech can also help you become a successful speaker. If you want to become an accomplished speaker you need to study other accomplished speakers. You need to pay attention to things like voice inflection. You need to hear how a good speaker will vary the pace of his remarks, how he will use dramatic pauses, and why and when his voice changes pitch. You need to be able to imitate these things. Listening to a talk multiple times can provide a good education in effective speaking.

LISTENING WHILE SELLING

Everything I am telling you about listening in seminars also applies when you are in someone's home trying to make a sale. You can mentally mimic your customers. I do not mean for you to sit in front of them and make the same face they are making. They will think you are making fun of them. What I mean is that you can position your body the way they have theirs positioned in order to feel what they are feeling.

Be an agnostic listener.

If I sit like the person I am talking to, I can pick up on what he or she is thinking. It is really kind of incredible. I can actually pick up on something unsaid just by putting myself in a mirroring posture. It not only gives you the feeling that you understand them, it actually allows you to understand them, at least up to a point.

I tell people to be agnostic listeners. An agnostic listener means that when you begin a conversation, you listen without a preconceived notion or belief of what the other person will say. You should not go into conversations, especially when trying to make a sale, with a bunch of preconceived notions in your head. You should not make too many assumptions or listen for answers to life's questions. Just listen to what the person you are talking to is saying, and be genuinely interested in what is being said.

MAKE YOUR CAR A ROLLING UNIVERSITY

Finally, use audio, such as tapes, MP3s, and CDs to educate and motivate yourself, just as you would with books.

Ask motivated business people how they spend their travel time, and they will tell you they listen to audio material. They actively listen to audios to maximize their time by learning, and they let good audios serve as personal mentors to motivate them.

Why is it that at a certain point in life people quit making money? Is it because they are tired and worn out? Or is it because they have lost their motivation? Audios can motivate you by developing your talents. They highlight skills and techniques that are proven to work.

Keep your brain productive.

Business-minded people, especially sales agents, spend a lot of time traveling. Using travel time to listen to audios makes this time worthwhile. It also serves to make traffic and wait-times a lot less stressful. If you vary your list of audios it will keep things fresh and interesting.

I have several success-building audios you can access and listen to for free on my website AndyAlbright.com/8steps.

Active listening should be diligently practiced. This habit will advance your career by sending a message to your customers that you have a sincere interest in them and not just the sale. It also tells management that you are eager to learn and want to excel in your business.

Pastor Mike Mitchner

Randy Woodson

Mike & Noelle Lewantowitz

Stephen & Hollie Davies

Dick Jenkins
K-Love Radio

CHAPTER 4

STEP FOUR:
READ

Whether you read one chapter a day or one page a day, you must read.

A wise, old man told me once that all the secrets of the universe were once kept in libraries that only an elite few could access. With access to these secrets, the elite few dominated the world.

Today, books are everywhere, even on-line. Anybody can have access to them. However, the wise, old man's words still apply today. Those who access ideas by reading will succeed over those who do not. The choice is yours. Choose to read!

An individual who can read but doesn't may as well be an individual who can't.

Every time I open a book, I learn something new, and you should, too. If you find yourself having trouble getting started, here is a prescription you can use to make yourself read. You may find it hard at first, but do it! Tear one page out of a book. Fold it up, and put it in your pocket. While at work, take it out and read it. It is illegal to tear up money, but there is nothing illegal about tearing up a book that you own. At first, it will feel odd because we are not accustomed to tearing up books. As children, we are taught not to tear up or mark in books. Put away those childish ways!

Also, if you are not accustomed to reading, it will feel odd for your brain to receive information from a source other than the television or radio. Even if it is just for 15 or 20 minutes a day, you must READ! If tearing pages from a book gets you to read just those pages, you have done better than if you would have let an intact book go unread.

READ AND RE-READ

I read a book, and then later I will read it again. If you were to pick up a book that I own, you would notice that it is highlighted in several colors. This is because I read books not just once, but several times. Each time I read a book—some as many as four or five times—I find something new and interesting. I learn something I did not know before. My highlights and notes reflect this.

> People who read—change. As they change, they cause those around them to change as well. They continue to grow and enrich their lives and those of others.

Successful people usually share a common trait: they are avid readers. They read everything— books, magazines, billboards, advertisements, and information from their competitors. Reading puts you ahead of the curve. By allowing books to become your mentors, your business will succeed because reading gives you knowledge, and knowledge gives you power.

The best book on reading I have ever read is *Read and Grow Rich* by Burke Hedges. (The old version of this book is *Read and Get Rich*). You should read it to learn the importance of reading. You can obtain a copy at AndyAlbright.com/burke.

READ TO SELL

If I want people in my organization to be successful in business, I trick them into reading. Yes, I am willing to trick people into becoming successful!

What I mean is this: If I see somebody consistently making the same mistakes, I can handle it one of two ways. I can tell them directly and forcibly, possibly jeopardizing the relationship, or I can point to a book that will convey the same message in a way more likely to be accepted and appreciated. That is my trick. The book is dispassionate, but it can light a fire under them and cause them to change for the better.

I like to get people fired up, and one way to do that is to get them to read success stories, as well as motivational books. As I commented earlier, if you want to get motivated, read the Robb Report and look at all the luxuries the world has to offer—everything from yachts and airplanes to fine furniture and jewelry. Realize the possibility of achieving enough success to own these things and you will get plenty motivated.

You should read about achievements of people like Warren Buffett or Bill Gates and see if it does not light a fire under you, knowing you are in a business with unlimited potential. If you do enough motivational reading you begin to line yourself up for achieving success as long as you follow through and do the other steps that are necessary to succeed.

> Employ your time in improving yourself by other men's writings so that you shall come easily by what others have labored hard for.
>
> –Socrates

I have made myself a resource to people seeking helpful reading material. People come to me and say, "What can I read to improve my listening skills?" Or, "What can I read to help my interpersonal skills?" I am like a "success" doctor in that I now have a "prescription" for almost any problem that comes up in business and sales. Do books work the way good prescriptions work? Absolutely! A book's ideas can change your thought patterns the way a prescription can change your metabolism.

I have seen people seeking motivation get "set on fire" by reading the right book. I use the term "set on fire" meaning to become enthusiastic and energized. It is interesting to me that the latest technological innovation is the Kindle, which is the new electronic book reader. I do not think it is any coincidence that the Kindle's creators chose a name that means to ignite or set afire. These geniuses obviously know that is exactly what reading does!

As valuable as listening is, reading provides even richer content. People talk too slowly to produce a whole lot of ideas in a short period. Books refine and condense speech, so you can get idea after idea onto a page. When reading, your brain moves rapidly, so energy builds like a fire gaining momentum. A book can change your belief system, and changing your belief system changes your activity. Changing your activity changes your results.

One of my best friends, Adam Katz, a former schoolteacher who is now a part of National Agents Alliance®, worked for many years for a set salary and never thought much about anything else being possible. He only began to open up to new possibilities by reading and re-reading important business books. His income is now 10 to 15 times what it once was, and he has achieved that in six or seven years, all because books changed his way of thinking. Quite an ironic turnaround for a teacher! Art Leazer, another friend and NAA® team member, will testify to the power of reading. He was the first NAA® team member to earn more than $1 million dollars in a year. He attributes his success to hard work and his dedicated focus to reading every day.

A change in thinking can be as important as learning the combination to a safe. If you were given information that four certain numbers were involved in a safe's combination, you would start by working those numbers in different patterns. But what if one of those numbers was wrong? You could combine numbers forever and you would never open the safe. Then someone comes along and gives you the right number to go with the other three. You would soon be inside that safe. That one piece of correct information will have made all the difference. The right change in your thinking can do the same thing.

A big difference in learning through listening and learning through reading is that a book demands your participation. You can listen passively and miss a lot of what is said, but a book is there to reveal information and ideas only when you actively engage with it. The ideas in a book's pages remain in place for you to re-read and reconsider.

So far, I have been talking mostly about motivational books and business books, both generic and specific. I am also a big believer in reading history and biography. History shows us where we come from and tends to show us who we are. Biographies show us the greatness that may lie within us, by showing how others achieved what they did. There is a world of good reading out there, and you must take advantage of it if you are going to succeed.

As for people who come up with excuses for not reading… Well, in my opinion there is no excuse. That is why reading is one of my *The 8 Steps to Success*. Remember, every step is required, not just recommended, to ensure your success.

Some people have never acquired the habit of reading. They have convinced themselves that they do not need to read. These are the ones to whom I make my recommendation of tearing out a page. I ask them if they are willing to invest as little as $18 dollars or $25 dollars in a successful career. I tell them to take that money and buy a book from my list. Then I tell them to tear a page from that book and read it. The idea scares them, like maybe they are doing something illegal. Tearing a page out of an $18 dollar investment seems to make reading that page almost necessary, so they read it. Then, they tear out another page and read that. You see, the value of a book is not in what it costs, or in its physical condition. The value of a book is in its reading, and what you acquire and implement from it, no matter how you go about it.

GET FIRED UP—FIRST BOOKS TO READ

- *Read and Grow Rich: How the Hidden Power of Reading Can Make You Richer in All Areas of Your Life*, Burke Hedges

- *Think and Grow Rich*, Napoleon Hill

- *How I Raised Myself from Failure to Success in Selling*, Frank Bettger

- *Acres of Diamonds*, Russell H. Conwell

- *The Go-Getter*, Peter B. Kyne

- T*he Greatest Salesman in the World*, Og Mandino

- *The 21 Indispensable Qualities of a Leader*, John C. Maxwell

- *Oh, The Places You'll Go*, Dr. Seuss

- *See You at the Top*, Zig Ziglar

- *The Greatest Miracle in the World*, Og Mandino

- *The Power of Positive Thinking*, Norman Vincent Peale

- *The Go-Giver: A Little Story About a Powerful Business Idea*, Bob Burg

- *How to Stop Worrying and Start Living*, Dale Carnegie

- *Training Camp*, Jon Gordon

- *Energy Bus*, Jon Gordon

- *The Positive Dog*, Jon Gordon

- *Millionaire Maker Manual*, Andy Albright

You're Rolling Now—2nd Wave of Books to Read

- *How to Win Friends and Influence People*,

Dale Carnegie

- *The Success Principles*, Jack Canfield
    - * (Pay close attention to the first chapter, "No Excuses")

- *The 7 Habits of Highly Effective People*, Stephen R. Covey

- *The Master Key to Riches*, Napoleon Hill

- *Developing the Leader Within You*, John C. Maxwell

- *Winning With People*, John C. Maxwell

- *Bringing Out the Best in People*, Alan Loy McGinnis

- *The Magic of Thinking Big*, David J. Schwartz

- *Success! The Glenn Bland Method*, Glenn Bland
    - * (Best book on setting goals, ever!)

Build a Team—Now You Can Have One

- *Developing the Leaders Around You*, John C. Maxwell

- *The 360-Degree Leader—Developing Your Influence*, John C. Maxwell

- *21 Irrefutable Laws Of Leadership: Revised & Updated*, John C. Maxwell

- *Millionaire Real Estate Agents*, Keller Williams
    - * Great book on building any business

- *Putting the One Minute Manager to Work*,
  Ken Blanchard & Robert Lorber

- *Soup*, Jon Gordon

- *The Seed*, Jon Gordon

- *No Complaining Rule*, Jon Gordon

Models to Build a Business With—Swipe and Deploy

- *The Purpose Driven Church*, Rick Warren
    * How to build a church or ANY organization!

- *Rich Dad, Poor Dad*, Robert T. Kiyosaki
    * How to make money the smart way

- *You Can't Steal Second With Your Foot on First*,
  Burke Hedges

- *Who Stole the American Dream?*, Burke Hedges

- *The Maxwell Leadership Bible*, John C. Maxwell

- *Making Vision Stick*, Andy Stanley

- *Wins, Losses and Lessons*, Lou Holtz

- *Leadership Gold*, John C. Maxwell

- *Good to Great*, Jim Collins
    * So many lessons in here

- *You, Inc.*, Burke Hedges

- *Go for No!*, Richard Fenton and Andrea Waltz

- *If You Don't Make Waves, You'll Drown,* Dave Anderson

- *Up Your Business,* Dave Anderson

- *Dream-Biz.com,* Burke Hedges

- *Millionaire Real Estate Agent,* Gary Keller

Best Relationship Books- Friendship Builders

- *How to Win Friends and Influence People,* Dale Carnegie

- *How to Have Confidence and Power in Dealing With People,* Les Giblin

- *Commitment to Love,* Deana McClary

- *The 17 Indisputable Laws of Teamwork,* John C. Maxwell

- *The 17 Essential Qualities of a Team Player,* John C. Maxwell

- *Cash Flow Quadrant,* Robert Kiyosaki

- *Skill With People,* Les Giblin

- *The Heart of a Tender Warrior,* Stu Weber

Getting Your Mind Right—Keep it on Track

- *How to Stop Worrying and Start Living,* Dale Carnegie

- Secrets of the Millionaire Mind: Mastering the Inner Game of Wealth, T. Harv Eker

- *Psycho-Cybernetics*, Maxwell Maltz

- *Getting Things Done*, David Allen

- *Awaken the Giant Within*, Anthony Robbins
    * Get ready for massive insights!

- *The Psychology of Winning*, Dr. Denis Waitley

- *The Difference Maker: Making Your Attitude Your Greatest Asset*, John C. Maxwell

- *Dare to Dream*, John C. Maxwell

- *Talent is Never Enough*, John C. Maxwell

- *The Ultimate Gift*, Jim Stovall

- *Hung by the Tongue*, Francis P. Martin

- *Eat that Frog! 21 Ways to Stop Procrastinating*, Brian Tracy
    * NOW!

- *Next Generation Leader*, Andy Stanley

- *Winning Every Day*, Lou Holtz

- *An Enemy Called Average*, John L. Mason

- *Reposition Yourself: Living Life Without*, T.D. Jakes

- *The Richest Man Who Ever Lived*, Steven K. Scott

- *Semper Fidelis*, Johnnie Clark

- *If You Don't Make Waves, You'll Drown,* Dave Anderson

- *The Go-Giver,* Bob Burg

- *How Successful People Think,* John C. Maxwell

- *Put Your Dream to the Test,* John C. Maxwell

- *The Friendship Factor,* Alan Loy McGinnis

Best Sales Books—Problem Solved

- *Missed Fortune 101,* Douglas Andrew

- *First Things First,* Stephen R. Covey, A Roger Merrill and Rebecca R. Merrill
  * This info applies to everything

- *Skill With People,* Les Giblin

- *The Art of Closing the Sale,* Brian Tracy

- *Teach Your Team to Fish,* Laurie Beth Hedges

- *The Parable of the Pipeline,* Burke Hedges

- *Fierce Conversations,* Susan Scott

Best Discipline Books—Straight and Narrow

- *Today Matters,* John C. Maxwell

- *Living Proof,* Clebe McClary

To print out your own list and for easy purchase of these books go to <u>AndyAlbright.com/booklist</u> or call 336-227-3319.

Jane & Haleigh

Venus Williams
World Champion Tennis Player

Bucky Waters

Eric Lindros
NHL Hockey Great

Wayne Goodwin
NC Insurance Commissioner

CHAPTER 5

STEP FIVE: ATTEND ALL MEETINGS

*I*t is important, and many successful people can tell you this, to attend all of the meetings that your company holds, be it sales meetings, seminars, or weekend conventions. This is especially true at National Agents Alliance®, where our training makes all the difference to our agents' selling and building success.

Meeting with the other members of the organization is also invaluable as a means of networking and learning from others.

> **Meetings and conventions trick business people into making money.**

When a person attends a meeting, he is sending a message that he wants to be a part of the organization. He desires to be a part of the team. He sees value in the organization's methods and he wants to benefit from them. Attending meetings allows a person to re-focus and re-direct his goals.

Imagine for a moment that you are a baseball player, a first baseman for the New York Yankees. An important game is coming up, but you tell your manager that you have to take off for an important family event. Reluctantly, the manager says okay, "I will put in a replacement." During your absence, the replacement hits two home runs. When you return after a couple of days, you are shocked that the manager has forgotten your name. You find yourself as the replacement for your replacement. That is what happened to Wally Pipp on June 2, 1925, who gave way to first baseman Lou Gehrig, who proceeded to play 2,130 consecutive games as the Yankees' first baseman. How about that for a "whoops!?"

Attending meetings generates enthusiasm and motivation. It initiates questions. Successful people are excited about attending meetings. They know meetings are a teaching mechanism,

Do not be selective in participation. Participate in all meetings and important events. Make no excuses.

designed to keep everyone informed about company products and services. They are a prime venue for networking with other agents and clients.

By creating opportunities for discussion, meetings provide information that will help you track performance, goals, and profitability. They help you learn how to sell through associating with others who are successful.

People get excited when they get outside their comfort zones, and meetings provide opportunities to get outside your comfort zone. Being removed from your comfort zone often creates the desire to "get up in there." If the meeting is about what you do, that is, if it is a sales meeting or a seminar on selling that should be reason enough to attend. These meetings are designed specifically to give you an edge in business, a head start against others who do what you do. If you are fighting to get ahead, to succeed beyond what you once knew was possible, you will take every opportunity that is offered to learn how. You will be fighting and scratching for information to make yourself successful.

If this is you, you are going to want to attend every meeting and take every opportunity to improve yourself that you can. This does not mean for you to become a meeting "groupie." Don't just attend to say that you went. Attend, takes notes, record it, learn, and do something! Too many people do not want success badly enough. They are doing OK, in their opinion, and they just want to stay in their comfort zone. Attending meetings, learning, actively listening, taking notes, paying attention, is just too much work for some. For others, however, it is more fuel for their fire.

So ask yourself: Do you want "just enough" or true success? Do you want to keep the bills paid, or do you want that second home, the ability to give to causes you believe in, that luxury automobile, or time to travel across the world with your family? What do you want?

MEET TO LEARN

In sales, it is important to put your ego aside and try to understand the needs of the person to whom you are selling. If a customer detects a sense of arrogance on your part, all of the logic and sales techniques in the world will not make him buy from you. This kind of understanding needs to carry over in all your business methods, and is especially important in your meeting attendance. If you do not believe that listening to the best people in the business telling you what they know will help you succeed, then you have allowed your ego and arrogance to get the best of you. You are denying yourself the help you need because of ego. If you are not smart enough or successful enough to lead sales meetings or to host seminars, then you should definitely be attending them.

I like to say that there are three ways to change your life: READ books, LISTEN to audio, and ASSOCIATE with successful people. I have talked about the importance of reading and listening to audios to gain knowledge.

Like books and audios, meetings are an important part of learning. Unlike reading books and listening to audios, meetings enhance learning by allowing you to use all of your senses. When you attend meetings, you hear the stories of successful individuals. You see the visual aids reflecting winning strategies for self-improvement. You touch the hands of effective leaders. It might be said that you can taste the enthusiasm of other people's desire to achieve and even smell the success you will experience with your new techniques and enthusiasm. You gain far more than written or spoken information when you are immersed in the experience of a good sales meeting, convention, or seminar.

Keep in mind that most of your senses are useless when your head is in the sand. The exact saying my good country friends use refers to having your head in another place. They say that four out of five of your senses will not work when your head is there! A good meeting or seminar lets you open up to learning by letting all of your senses get involved in the learning process.

ONLY LOSERS COMPLAIN

People who do not want to attend meetings always justify staying home. They often say: "It costs too much," or "It will take too much time away from my family." In fact, they do not want to see the value of making the effort to attend. These people have the least success in our business, because they do not want to put out the extra effort. By not attending meetings, they are not only failing to take step five of *The 8 Steps to Success*, they are also backing away from step two, because they are failing to undertake some very important work.

Keep this in mind: The people who attend all of the meetings never complain about them. It is only the people who refuse to benefit from meetings who complain about them. The complainers are the ones who are losing by not taking the opportunity to learn, and it is these losers who justify in their minds that they are not missing anything. Therefore, they think they do not need to attend. They miss out on the true value of attending meetings. By attending meetings you are "tricking yourself" into making money and becoming successful. You are providing yourself with opportunities that motivate you to adopt methods you might never have tried otherwise.

GROW TO KNOW, GO TO GROW

Meetings and conventions allow you to meet face-to-face with individuals and make direct contact with them. Meetings also allow you to learn from those "who are in the hunt" and are experiencing success. Nothing is more essential to real learning.

The Greek philosopher Plato taught that personal contact was the essence of teaching. Do you remember having a schoolteacher who really made a subject come alive for you? One who really lit up your imagination and made you want to learn? Now, try thinking of a computer-instructed course you might have taken. Did it ever give you the same sense of excitement? Direct contact is what meetings, conventions, and seminars are all about. They open you up to success by getting you excited about making sales.

Telephone conversations or electronic communications simply do not provide the same value. They lack the personal contact that is so important when creating relationships and exchanging ideas. If you are not face-to-face, you have no eye contact. You do not get the same information you can get from observing another's body language. In short, it is hard to form a relationship with a person when you are not face-to-face with that person.

How many times have you heard somebody on the radio for years and then been surprised at the way they looked when you saw him or her in person? How many times has the same thing happened when you first met somebody you had only spoken with on the telephone? In both cases, you had developed an incorrect mental image that may even have clouded your opinion of this person. Direct contact creates the opportunity to form a relationship because it makes it personal. Paying attention to the speakers at meetings and seminars, and by watching how top performers behave, even during breaks, can also teach you techniques and provide you with communication skills to success.

Remember what I said in step three about mimicking people's facial expressions and about reading what people are thinking by imitating their body language? Use your time in meetings not just to learn from what people are saying but also to learn how they say it. Watching the speakers in meetings is an excellent way to learn about which communication methods are effective and which are not.

If you knew with 100% certainty that attending all company meetings would make you rich, would you go?

I make a conscious effort to learn about communication from seminar speakers. I will even pick up on the body language of a person I know is successful and imitate it later without even understanding why. If it is working for him, I will put it into play until I understand why it is working for him, and by then, it is working for me.

Competing for your upline's time is vital to your success. Do not give him the opportunity to overlook your potential and move on to someone else.

Every year our organization holds a national convention. I hold a contest among our managers to see how many agents they can recruit to come to the event. Why do I do this? Because I have seen, year after year, that the success of an organization directly corresponds to its national convention attendance. It is when people commit to building relationships that they stay in the organization long-term. People who have never met the others in their organization have no sense of belonging. Everyone likes to feel as if they belong to something.

Immediately following every NAA® convention, the number of people writing business increases. I know that whichever manager promotes the convention most effectively will be the manager who brings the most people to the convention. His will be the agency with long-term sustained growth. When the top 30 agents or managers in our organization are selected, one thing common to them all is the number of people they have attending the convention. Fact, the top 30 always have the most people to attend the annual convention. It is simply a fact.

Also, meetings allow you to make a positive impression. Putting a face to a name makes a person recognizable. It stores an individual in your memory bank. Months down the road, you may find yourself saying, "Yes, I remember you. I met you at the National Convention. We had a conversation and it totally changed my business. It changed my life!"

Face-to-face contacts leave a lasting impression, so remember to leave a favorable impression. Think through the image you will present. Are you dressed in professional attire? Are you using eye contact? Are you speaking intelligently or are you rambling? First impressions are lasting impressions. Make sure yours is always a good one.

Attending meetings gives you credibility with upline management. If your upline instructs you to be present at a weekly sales meeting at 8 a.m., be there at 7:45 a.m. Do not be late. Do not call at 7:55 a.m. and say that you are running behind because you are having car trouble. Be respectful of others' time.

Meetings allow you to associate with successful people. People's energy and motivation levels are contagious. Associate yourself with positive attitudes rather than with individuals with negative attitudes. Successful people surround themselves with successful people. You cannot stay hot if you do not stay close to the fire!

The speakers we have at our meetings are the most successful among us. Listen to what they have to say. Observe how they handle themselves when speaking. Imitate what you see in their facial expressions and body language. Be sure to use the time between speakers to meet them to ask questions. Use free time to talk with other successful agents. What an opportunity to learn! Get your head out of the sand!

Lastly, consider your organization. If, for you, meetings are the least effective means of the three main learning methods—if you're more of a reader or listener, consider that your organization is made up of different types of people. So, even if you find meetings less effective for yourself than reading and listening to digital recordings, attend all meetings as an encouragement to those in your downline who might find them the most effective way to learn. Remember, part of your job is to lead. Make sure the people following you are learning all they can by your example.

Successful people are driven, motivated, energetic, and positive thinkers. They are winners. If you do not associate yourself with winners, how can you expect to win?

Some great motivators to watch, whether you like them or not, include:

- Bill Cowher—Former Pittsburgh Steelers Coach

- Donald Trump—Real Estate Mogul

- Lou Holtz—Former Head Football Coach

- Joel Osteen—Author and Minister

- Rick Warren—Author and Minister

- Oprah Winfrey—Media Mogul

- John C. Maxwell—Author and Speaker

- Dave Anderson—Author & Motivational Speaker

- Jon Gordon—Best-selling Author

- Brian Tracy—Author and Speaker

- Andy Andrews—Author and Speaker

Take advantage of learning from people like these by attending their seminars. Take advantage of what National Agents Alliance® has to offer by attending all of our meetings. There is so much to be gained and so little to lose. It is a necessary step to success.

Albright Family
Christmas 2011

Lauren Nelson
Miss America 2007

Douglas Andrews
Author—Missed Fortune

Curtis Strange

Darwin Hurme
VP, Foresters

CHAPTER 6

STEP SIX:
BE TEACHABLE

*P*eople change when they want to change. If you change fast, that indicates you want to change. If you change slowly, that indicates you do not want to change. Being teachable means that you want to change and that you are willing to change fast. You are looking for something better. Put people in your organization who want to change and you will look like a genius. You have to become a good "finder" of people and a good judge of character. People will give you credit for changing people, and all you did was find people who wanted to change.

It took a long time for me to become teachable, and the change was a gradual one. I fought changing until I was about 35 years old. Only then did I really start becoming successful.

People overestimate the power of a few words from a coach, but they underestimate the power of ongoing coaching.

Just think how much faster my success might have come if I had learned to change when I was in my 20s! What if I had learned early on to be more teachable instead of thinking I was smarter than everyone else?

Missing out on those years of success is what has made me so adamant about people learning to be teachable—especially young people—without spending too much time fighting it. I needed proof, and it took example after example before I finally figured things out. If you will take my word that this step, Be Teachable, is absolutely necessary for success, and you act on it, you can move forward a lot faster and with a lot less pain than I did.

LEARN OR LOSE

Speed up your growth. Be an accelerator. Time, money, and emotion are invested resources. The longer it takes you to change, the more time, money and emotion you are wasting. Do you want results in your life? Do you want to change your life? If the answer is yes, be willing to make the necessary sacrifices to change, to invest your time, money, and emotions to achieve results.

An example in my life of learning to be teachable dates back to when I was a kid. I was very impatient, and I had a temper. When we played sports, I would get mad and blow up at a teammate if I thought he was doing something wrong. I even ran over a little girl who was playing football with us. I got impatient with something she did, and I just knocked her down and ran right over her.

My daddy was watching us play and saw me do it. Now my daddy had cautioned me about my temper a dozen times, but this time, the time I ran over the little girl, he brought the point home to me with his belt. It took some pain, but I learned to control my temper better that day. If I had been teachable by nature, I could have learned to control it by listening to my father long before he had to use his belt on me. If you are teachable, you can change before your mistakes cause you pain!

BE A GENIUS!

If you are with National Agents Alliance®, and you are putting people into your organization, remember to choose people who want to change over people who are slow to learn. Everybody loves it when a slow learner finally "gets it" and changes, but you can expend a lot of time and energy with slow learners. In the same amount of time you spent with one slow learner, you could have found half a dozen fast learners who make your job much easier.

Everybody loves an underdog, but you do not build a

championship team with a bunch of underdog players. Everybody loves the movie *Rudy*, and everybody cheers when he gets into the game against Georgia Tech, but Notre Dame never won a championship with a bunch of "Rudys." You, too, will never build a winning team with all "Rudys."

If you cannot change your people fast. Change your people—fast!

People often like to credit me with working miracles because I change people. They witness me working with people and the people become successful, and then they think I am a genius. All I do, in most cases, is find the people that are ready to change. It is as much about looking for the people who will do The 8 Steps as it is about selling The 8 Steps.

OVERCOME TO BECOME

How do you see yourself? What is your vision? The book of Proverbs states, "Where there is no vision, my people perish," Proverbs 29:18, KJV. Being teachable and capable of change gives purpose to your life. It gives you direction. Consider that every time you steer off a correct path by one degree and continue on, you keep compounding the distance between the correct path and where you are going the longer you continue. Over a few hours, days, and weeks, that one degree takes you wider and wider of the true path. In the short run, there is not much of a variation, but over time the difference between the "right" path and the "wrong" course will become greatly exaggerated.

With constant correction and guidance, you constantly correct your course. By watching what you are doing, and by listening to somebody who sees you getting off course, you can always make a correction. You have to be open to what a good mentor can show you, though. You have to be teachable, and willing to change your direction when necessary.

If you are teachable it means that you are ready, willing, and able to change. You must be ready to accept the challenge and sacrifices that change demands. I challenge you to get rid of the useless and harmful habits in your life, the habits that do not lend themselves to your success. Now is the time to make a decision to change your life. You have the artillery to attack. The only thing holding you back is you.

Developing the mindset to become a winner must come from deep within you. I can tell you to find the passion, the drive, and the ambition to find success, but you must internalize this information. You must find your own reason for doing so, the why of changing your life. Why will you get up early to work? Why will you attend meetings? Why will you be ready to change? Find the reason. Every individual's why is different.

PUT YOUR GAME PLAN IN PLACE

Life is not a game to be played. Life is a series of events that can be planned. Do you see your life ahead? Do you have a vision? At the Walt Disney World ribbon-cutting ceremony in Orlando, Florida in 1971, Walt Disney's brother, Roy and Walt's wife, Lily commented on Walt's vision for the theme park. Roy said:

> *"He was really, in my opinion, truly a genius-creative, with great determination, singleness of purpose, and drive; and through his entire life, he was never pushed off his course or diverted by other things."*

Even though Walt Disney died a few years prior to the opening of Walt Disney World, his vision was carried out. He had shared this vision with others in his organization, who then made it their own. When a reporter asked Walt's brother if he thought it was sad that Walt Disney never got to see the completed park, his brother smiled and said, "He saw it in his dreams 1,000 times."

You have to be able to put your game plan into place. Walt Disney did this so effectively his game plan was carried out even after his death. As Barry Clarkson says, "Even your excuses have to be reasons." Barry always used his children as a reason to succeed, not as an excuse to avoid working hard. When you make this directional change, you will change your life, and you will change the lives of others around you.

Learning something new should be a daily part of your life. Make it a practice to write things down. You should record conference calls. Think and process new information. Do not make important decisions without consulting people you trust. Being teachable means you can act on what you learn. Use what you learn in ways that will grow your income and grow your business. By becoming more growth-oriented, you will find yourself never satisfied. Growth can be defined as a continual process of learning. For this reason, it is more important to be more growth-oriented than goal-oriented.

LEARN AS YOU GO

Always look for means of self-improvement. Sometimes this means taking a step back and gathering your energies. Stephen Covey says that you need to "sharpen your saw." In his book *The 7 Habits of Highly Effective People,* Covey lists ways to personal renewal, such as exercise, meditation, education, and organization, Covey, 1998.

Once you have gathered your energies, set a game plan, begin with the end in mind, but then work that plan step by step. Remember, you cannot go through the entire process at once. You do not even have to understand the whole process at the beginning. Just do what needs to be done, every day. Follow the instructions. Follow *The 8 Steps to Success.*

I have always enjoyed playing Monopoly. Everybody, it seems, has played Monopoly at one time or another. Do you remember seeing that list of rules printed on the bottom of the box-top? Fortunately, most people first play Monopoly with people who have already played it. If you first tried playing by opening the box and reading all the rules, you would probably just close the box again. However, you do not have to understand all the rules before you start playing the game. Count out the money, roll the dice and start moving. When you need guidance, look it up in the rules. Monopoly is not hard work. In fact, it is fun, that is why you play it. Business, while it requires work, does not have to be as hard as people make it. Business can be fun, and success is certainly fun! Just follow those rules that apply each day and be teachable as you go along.

The idea of learning as you go and working a process step by step has never been as clear to me as when my wife was diagnosed with cancer. The situation seemed impossible for us to grasp at first. The whole process seemed complicated because we had no idea how to go about it. We were not doctors. What did we know? What did the doctors even know? Then, as I have related, her doctor told us that if we followed the instructions, Jane could reach remission of cancer and over time, be cured!

We soon found out that the rules for Jane's recovery were fairly simple: Attend all Meetings was one, as in do not miss any chemotherapy sessions. Eating healthy foods was one. (Imagine that! People with cancer should eat healthy foods!) Just follow the steps, ALL the steps, as they are laid out. We did not get to choose which steps we liked! Of course, we did all the steps, and Jane has been cancer free for 20 years now.

Now, what if we would have ignored the instructions thinking that cancer was so big and scary that getting Jane well was something we could not accomplish? Some people look at cancer just that way. Others think they can get well on their own terms, and they do not listen to the experts. Both types lessen their chances for recovery. Many people do the same thing in life. They lessen their chance for success, either because they refuse to engage in the right process or prefer their own misguided way. These people are not teachable. You cannot be slow to change where your health and your success are concerned.

WHAT KEEPS YOU FROM BEING TEACHABLE?

The biggest impediment to becoming teachable, in my experience, is the influence of other people. I have talked about the value of association: that is, being around and learning from the right people. Unfortunately, associating with the wrong people can have the opposite effect: preventing you from achieving.

There is an old lesson about crabs in a bucket. If you catch a crab and put it into a bucket, it will have no trouble getting out. It can raise itself high enough to stretch out a claw and grab the rim of the bucket. Then it will pull itself up and out. With one crab, you have to put a lid on the bucket to keep it from getting out.

Once you've caught a second crab, though, you can pretty much do away with the lid. Two or more crabs will pull each other back down trying to climb over each other to get out. As soon as one tries to get out, another pulls him back down trying to do the same thing.

Associating with negative people is like being a crab in a bucket with other crabs. Nothing is more detrimental to you as you try to learn to work *The 8 Steps to Success* than associating with people who tell you The 8 Steps will not work. Or, they may say selling insurance is "not right for you," or that owning your own business only works for certain people and you are not one of them.

If your spouse is negative regarding your career, you have a real problem. That is why recruiting National Agents Alliance® agents means getting both the agent and his or her spouse committed. Both people need to be on board or the agent will be like a crab always being pulled back into a bucket.

If you are trying to succeed, stay clear of people who do not want you to be successful. In every seminar I lead, I get personal very quickly. I tell you, and everyone in the audience who is there to learn, to take out a sheet of paper and write down the names of three people you should spend less time around. I want people to think of the three people they now associate with who are negative influences on them, people who will try to talk them out of learning something new, like how to obtain wealth or start a new business. Too often, these people are family members, which is sad, but if it is true, you still need to put them on the list and you need to spend less time around them.

If you feel bad about this, think of it this way. Often, these people just want something from you anyway. You probably sense this, and you probably give them a pretty small Christmas gift each year.

So do this: triple the size of the Christmas gift you give them next year, but spend less time around them. See if they are not happier about the bigger gift than they are sad about not being around you. Think about it, will this person be happier with the gift than with the time spent with you? You are probably going to decide they would be happier with the gift.

Next I will tell you, take out another sheet of paper and write down the names of three people you need to spend more time around. Once you have decided who they are, you need to find ways to spend more time with them. Part of the reason for spending less time around the first three people is that doing so will give you more time to spend around these three. Spending less time around the first three can be a simple as hitting "ignore" when their number pops up on your cell phone. You know that part about changing? Doing this is a real simple way you can change.

At the next seminar, your list of three people to spend more time around is going to change if you have made a real effort to get around the first three. Inconvenience yourself to get around the right people. Be like the kid in the movies who hides out in the clubhouse locker room and caddies to be around the pro golfers, and then becomes a pro golfer himself.

Be teachable. Don't think you are too smart to learn, and don't think you're too dumb to achieve.

I have booked flights knowing somebody I wanted as a mentor was taking it. I asked him first if he would mind, then I sat with him on the plane. If someone you want to meet has written a book, read his book. Then, if he is giving a seminar, go to it, and get there early to meet him.

Get out of your comfort zone and change. Do not be like I was and decide that the way you are is the way you are, or that you are too smart to learn. I have to admit that some of those who I thought were the least intelligent people in our organization have turned out to be the highest achievers. I never want to be so smart that I cannot be successful!

Stephen Davies is one of NAA®'s team players who immediately adjusted who he associated with and as a result he became the youngest agent to earn more than $1 million dollars in one year at the age of 25. He is a shining example of the power of being teachable.

BREAK THE CHAIN

Child abuse is a horrific situation, as we all know. One of the saddest things about abuse is that it is often passed on: the abused person grows up to victimize another child. A milder form of abuse consists in people being told they are not smart enough or do not have a fair chance at success. No one has done this or that in their family, and so they should not expect to be any different.

I am thankful I was never held back like that by my parents. I have talked about how my mother encouraged me just by telling other people that I could be counted on to do whatever it was I said I would do. As far as she was concerned, I could achieve anything I wanted. I grew up thinking I could do anything because my parents always encouraged me, and I never have had that little voice in my head that constantly says, "no, you can't."

If you have been limited by others, by family or anyone else, make a decision to break the chain. Let yourself be the last one to be limited, by overcoming your limitations. Learn to change and pass that on. Be teachable, and then teach others. In Stephen Davies case, he first became successful with NAA® and then in turn helped his parents become successful. This is a terrific example of breaking the chain in a big way!

Tony Hardee

*John Maxwell
2007*

Bridget & Ryan Phelps

*Kyle Wyley
Country Music Star*

Bob Ryan

CHAPTER 7

STEP SEVEN:
BE ACCOUNTABLE

What does it mean to be accountable? In simple terms, it means you do what you say you are going to do. You are who you say you are. As my friend, Vietnam hero Clebe McClary, says, "Say what you mean and mean what you say." Doing what you say you will do may sound easy, but many people find it extremely difficult. To see how you are doing with this, have a trusted friend tell you whether you follow through on your promises. Do your actions reflect what you say to other people?

If a police officer pulls you over and asks if you know how fast you were going, do you say, "I don't know, over 40?" trying to cloud the issue? Or, do you say, "Sir, I was going 52 miles per hour." Be accountable for your actions, both good and bad. In doing so, you will become more committed to your goals.

> "There are two primary choices in life: Accept conditions as they exist, or accept the responsibility for changing them."
>
> –Denis Waitley

Being accountable requires being committed in all areas of your life. Not only must you work, you must also prepare FOR work. A professional baseball player is committed to playing baseball full-time. In order to be accountable in his work, he must also commit himself to a life of watching his diet and exercise. He must assume the responsibility of all his commitments, including, because of his public status, setting a good example with his behavior.

One easy way to remember what being accountable means is to think in fiscal terms. When you are accountable, you account for your actions as you account for your family's money or funds that have been entrusted to your care. Think of yourself as a CPA of your time, talent, and behavior.

When you sign your name to a check, you attest that there is money in your account to back it up. When you schedule an appointment, treat it as if you are writing a check that says you will show up. Neither type of check should ever bounce. No excuses!

I remember attending a seminar where the speaker showed up on time even though his schedule had gone terribly awry. He had to charter a plane and make other expensive arrangements in order to arrive at the seminar as promised. I am sure he lost money on the deal, but losing money on the engagement was a lot less important than following through and keeping his good name.

Any organization that you create will inevitably follow your lead regarding work habits. You have to be accountable or your organization will become worthless and fall apart. If you are not accountable, how are people going to follow you? This is true for customers as well as for your staff and your organization. Any time you come across as a person who does not follow through, or is not accountable, others start losing confidence and trust in that person. This loss of confidence, trust, and accountability often leads to a loss of sales.

90-Day Challenge

Do you wake up every morning feeling comfortable in your lifestyle? The attitude of successful individuals is never an attitude of complacency. Make a commitment to yourself over the next 90 days to change your attitude and to hold yourself accountable for your actions and your words. Commit yourself, like the Rotary Club motto, to "never criticize, condemn or complain."

Edify your thoughts and you will edify your actions.

Always position yourself to operate from a position of strength, not a position of weakness. This will require, again, commitment. Your biggest enemy is your own mind. If you are always thinking negatively, when will you find the time to think positively? Commit and change. Be responsible for your actions. Rather than taking two steps forward and three steps back, reverse the downward spiral and make your life into one of constant forward movement.

Do not lie to yourself. Setting goals is important, but make sure your goals are the logical outcome of an attainable game plan. Do not set impossible or unlikely goals for yourself that you will have to back off of when you see they cannot be attained. Let your goals be promises to yourself, and only make promises you know you can keep.

One thing I learned early in my career was to only make promises I knew I could keep. It sounds great to a customer when you promise the moon and stars…until you fail to deliver them! The customer is putting his trust in you. If you say you will deliver, he has a right to expect delivery. Do not say things you do not mean and do not promise what you are not sure you can deliver. It hurts your self-confidence, because not only does the customer or your organization see your lack of accountability, you see it, too.

DEVELOP YOUR FAITH/ ACCOUNTABILITY MUSCLE

The Bible tells us that even a small amount of faith, faith the size of a mustard seed, can work wonders. The same is true of accountability. It is OK if you begin with faith or accountability in a small way.

When you are new to something, when you first take something on faith, or when you start actively practicing accountability, you have to start out small. The whole business of positioning yourself through accountability means doing what I call building your faith muscle. You might also consider it in terms of building your accountability muscle.

When developing a business, you have to develop character. You are constantly going to be making promises and setting goals. The trick is to make realistic (often small) promises and to always deliver on them. Make short-term, attainable goals and then reach these on your way to achieving attainable long-range goals.

Have faith even if it is just a small faith in small things. Doing small things right every time develops your faith muscle and lets you see that you can do more than you thought. Be accountable by delivering on every small promise you make, and you will see that you can deliver more and more. Then, make bigger promises and take on bigger commitments when you know you are able to follow through, and feel that muscle grow.

It is like lifting weights. You might set out to get strong enough to lift a certain weight, like being able to bench-press your body weight. Or, you may just want to see how far you can develop yourself by how much you can eventually lift. You achieve your weight-lifting goal by starting with a weight you can comfortably handle and lifting it repeatedly, until you gradually develop muscles that can lift a slightly heavier weight. Then, you lift that weight repeatedly and move up again. You may want to lift 200 pounds by next week, but do not tell yourself you are going to do it and then find out that it is impossible. Develop slowly by lifting weights you can handle.

Just remember, being accountable starts with finding out what you can handle. Then, you follow through because you can. You eventually see how being accountable in small things leads to being accountable in bigger things. Being consistently accountable gives you vision. It is a good feeling!

CREATE A POSITIVE OUTLOOK— CREATE A POSITIVE OUTCOME

I talk a lot about the time my wife, Jane, was diagnosed with Hodgkin's Disease, and how we, especially she, dealt with it. As

I have said, we were young at the time, and Jane was teaching science full-time in a middle school. From the very beginning of this nightmare, Jane's attitude was positive. Never once did I hear her complain about the treatments, the nausea, and the hair loss. Never once did I hear her complain about commuting to Wake Forest Baptist Hospital in Winston-Salem, N.C. for chemotherapy and radiation. Never once did she complain that she had to continue working because we were struggling to pay our bills. She never let her mind be filled with negative thoughts or a negative outcome. Jane's positive attitude, her consistent faith that God was in charge, carried us through this medical crisis. Jane had developed a strong faith muscle, which she exercised by following her doctors prescribed course of treatment—through being accountable.

Fear produces negative results. Appreciation and thankfulness produce positive results..

Today, Jane remains cancer-free after 20 years. Even though the doctors warned her that the chemotherapy drugs could leave her unable to have children, we now have two healthy, beautiful children. Jane decided in her mind that cancer was not going to overtake her life. By creating a positive outlook, she created a positive outcome.

She always looked to God, and now gives Him 100 percent of the credit for her recovery, but she also never lost sight of the fact that she was responsible for her own actions. She committed to the treatments, to making herself well, and to overcoming this pothole in our road by moving forward. Also, she relied on me to be her partner. Never once did our attitude waiver because we knew this was our fight and we were in it to win. We would not settle for anything but a victory. I do not know of any stronger individual than Jane. She said from day one she was going to beat this deadly disease, and she did. She committed to what was required to make herself well, and she made herself accountable for what happened to her and to her family.

Jane's father passed away late within the same year of Jane's diagnosis and treatment. She now views her illness as a blessing in disguise because it allowed her to spend extra time with her dad that she would not have had otherwise.

Make yourself accountable for your life. Commit yourself to find the positive and eliminate the negative in your life. Your outlook WILL determine your outcome!

Phil Falcone

Jim Henson

The Roberts Family

Debbie Yow

Andy's 1st
Big Commitment

CHAPTER 8

STEP EIGHT: COMMUNICATE WITH A POSITIVE MENTAL ATTITUDE

Y our ability to communicate conveys a message about your personality. Are you constantly finding reasons to complain? Are you ridiculing or finding fault in your co-workers and friends? Communication can be destructive or constructive.

In the movie *Cool Hand Luke*, Paul Newman struggles against authority. Strother Martin tells him that if he wanted to get along in prison he needed "to get [his] mind right." What else did Martin say to him? "What we have here...is a failure...to communicate." We all love Luke for standing up to the prison guards, but by "failing to communicate," Luke did not make it out of the movie alive.

Make a conscious decision that you are not going to complain. Resolve as well that you are going to ask questions far more often than making statements. If you ask questions, it tells others that you are anxious to learn and that you are interested in what they have to say. Positive communication indicates your desire to be of service. Communicating in a positive manner will lure people into your business.

A successful business is a contagious attraction. Either you bring individuals toward you, or you push them away.

Let us take, as an example, an insurance agent on an appointment. The agent begins by picking up on an easily identifiable object in the client's home or office. "I see from your family photos that you are a grandmother." Then he transitions and takes action: "I have insurance policies that will cover all the members of your family." Next, he communicates a positive evaluation of his customer. "I know you want to make sure your family is protected if something were to happen to you." Finally, he builds credibility by showing that he believes in the benefits of his business: "I bought the same policy for myself, my wife, and my 4-year-old daughter." You form a connection with your customers when you have similarities with them, or when you share common interests. Use what you have in common to your advantage by talking about it with your customers!

Projecting a positive mental attitude is something that can be learned, just like anything else. I read recently about a guy who said, "The first thing I try to do when I wake up in the morning and I do not feel dirt pressing down on me is get excited. I start thinking I am lucky. I have got a chance!" This man has learned to appreciate what he has. He starts off each day appreciating life itself. Now that is a positive mental attitude!

So, what do you have to complain about? You woke up alive this morning, did you not? Remember: Light and dark cannot coexist. Negative and positive cannot coexist. Train yourself to get past the negatives in your life and fill those spaces with positives. If you can get excited about being alive, it is hard for you to fret over that meeting you have coming up. You will have to deal with negative things as they come up each day, but right now you have positive momentum. Every day when you wake up, you should get that positive momentum going. Your whole organization fell apart? Everyone quit on you? Try this: "You know what? I am glad I am alive so that I can rebuild my organization!"

It's How You Say It

Choosing the right means of communicating is also important. If your message is factual, communicate with an e-mail or a text message. Telephone numbers, sales figures, and contacts are facts. If your message involves emotions, communicate with a phone call or in person. Thoughts, ideas, and comments always stir up others' emotions, and in-person meetings, and to a lesser degree the telephone, help you sense how the person is responding. Use the most effective means of communication for the type of message you have to relay.

It is also important to consider the tone of your communication. Not all communication is positive, yet all communication can be relayed in a positive manner. Management needs information, both positive and negative, when it affects business. They need to know whenever there are problems. They need to be kept informed of ongoing situations or areas where trouble may occur. However, these things should be conveyed in the most positive context possible.

For example, the statement, "We have a situation with our turnaround time on application submittals," relays a negative situation in a positive tone. "You had better fix our turnaround time in application submittals, or we are going to lose customers," presents the same problem as a personal accusation. To which would you respond more positively?

Are you tearing down or building up?

Communicate your facts and emotions with a positive tone. Communication should always use inclusive words like "we" and "our" rather than "you" or "they." By using inclusive language, problems within an organization become the whole team's problem, instead of an individual's problem. As a member of the team, you are not accusing others of inadequacies. Instead, you are addressing a situation that needs to be addressed by the whole team, yourself included.

DO NOT TELL ME YOUR PROBLEMS

If you have started out positively by being appreciative about just being alive, you are way ahead of a lot of people. If you can take that positive momentum into your day, you are going to project a positive mental attitude. If you do not have positive momentum, how are you going to project positivity?

Please do not come to me and tell me things are not good, even if you have a lot that is going wrong. Start off talking to me about how you woke up and breathed the air and it felt good. If you have got to tell me something negative, you can get around to that, but start with something positive. That way we will be as positive about the negative as we can once we get to it. Remember what Mary Poppins told the kids in the movie: "Just a spoonful of sugar helps the medicine go down." Give me the bad news with a little bit of sugar. Be positive in getting through the negative. Keep the *positive* end in mind. Speaking of movies, one of my favorites is *The Shawshank Redemption*. Here you have a guy in prison working toward a way out. It takes him 30 years, but he never gives up. Where does he end up? On a beach in Mexico! He ends up *not* in prison and he ends up wealthy and doing very well. Talk about keeping a positive attitude!

Remember, the glass is neither half full nor half empty. It is always full. It is full of water and air.

I am not being naïve about this. I know life is full of failure and negative experiences. I am very much against wearing rose-colored glasses, but I am also very big on starting out the day by being happy about the fact that I am still breathing!

THE BAD MAKES THE GOOD

One thing I have learned is that you will not have good days without bad days. Bad days are actually important. They provide a comparison and allow you to appreciate the good days.

The seeds of success are planted in the obstacles of distress. It is important to build on obstacles. They can be the foundation of your success if you build on them instead of letting them destroy you. Make every obstacle or crisis an opportunity to get better.

A lot of people actually thrive in a crisis and do well under pressure. A crisis gets them going. Being positive, on the other hand, tends to lessen the frequency and severity of crises. You should get excited about the obstacles, because once you cut down on the crises in your life, you cannot rely on the adrenaline they provide to give you momentum.

Here is how I look at positives and negatives when dealing with agents in my organization. If an agent has had something positive happen, he first has to recognize it. Too many people let the day's positive experiences get lost in the day's negative experiences. Let's say I'm talking to an agent and he tells me he made 72 calls and had two positive responses. He is depressed. Two out of 72. What he needs to recognize is that it is not just two out of 72. What he needs to recognize is that he has achieved two positive responses! Once he is looking at it that way, he is a thousand times more likely to improve his score to four, then eight, then 36 out of 72!

Please do not tell me you made 72 calls and only got two sales. Just tell me you got two sales. Then we can talk about how you got them and how you are going to get more of them.

Statistics are just statistics. It is how you look at them that determines everything. How you look at statistics determines your energy level, which determines your activity level, with determines your success level. If two out of 72 looks like a negative to you and your statistics are two sales in 72 calls, then you are looking at a negative, and you are depressed about your business. If, on the other hand, two sales is a good thing, then your energy level will rise and your success rate will, too. Momentum is built by evaluating your statistics positively. Being positive allows you to see what you did right amidst everything you may have done wrong. Once you grasp why things went right, you can replicate those actions and multiply your success.

Simply put, if you can be positive and convey a positive attitude, the "misses" are going to become as positive to you as the "hits." If you are learning from the misses, you are getting more hits. So, now it is like the glass that is always full. Which are the negatives, the misses or the hits? Neither, if the misses are positives. If air is as important to your life as water, then which is the negative half of the glass? The half with the water or the half with the air?

It's a Business of Attraction

How many times have you found yourself "sizing someone up" before the first words have been spoken? All of us do this.

Before introductions are made, and before anyone has shaken hands, people form opinions of each other, which is why personal presentation is so important. Each of us communicates an image of who we are by the way we look and act.

Business requires personal attraction. Everything you communicate, verbally or otherwise, either brings individuals toward you or pushes them away. By presenting yourself in a positive manner, you pull individuals into your circle and make them favorably disposed toward your agenda. So, you need to constantly ask yourself, "Am I advancing or hindering my growth? Am I bringing people in or am I pushing people away?" Are people glad to be around you, or are they glad when you go away? I have a friend I call by the nickname "Sunshine." He brightens up a room just by leaving it!

Dress for Success

Personal appearance conveys attitude. It tells others you are confident and in control, or it tells them you are uncertain and nervous. Appearance can either build or destroy that first positive mental impression. When you approach someone, are you smiling, or are your lips locked tight in anticipation of grandma's cough medicine? Is your suit freshly pressed, or did you dig it up off the floor in the back of your closet? Can you see your reflection in your shoes, or do your shoes look like they were shined with a brick?

Dress for Success. Your personal appearance is a reflection of who you are. Relax your brow. Take your keys and your change out of your pocket. Smile...not a fake, smirking grin, but a genuine, whole-hearted smile. Show your customer you want to be there. Demonstrate to your customer and organization that you are a professional. Convey an attitude of professionalism. How you present yourself will form a lasting impression before you ever open your mouth.

We have all heard the cliché, "You never get a second chance to make a first impression." The reason we have heard it is because it is true. Use your personal appearance to your advantage, not to your disadvantage. If you are ever uncertain of the appropriate dress for a meeting or event, ask someone what to wear!

LINE UP YOUR WORDS

The words you use have a major impact on how others see you. Are your words lining up with who you are and where you want to go, or are your sentences filled with "Uh…uh…uh," and "you know?" You may have graduated at the top of your class, but when it comes to speaking, do you stumble over your words and ramble? Think before you speak. Line your words up with your thoughts!

It is important to remember to communicate about tomorrow, not yesterday. Your manager does not want to hear about the past; they want to know what you have to say about the future. Consider this comment, "I have a great sales presentation I would like to share with you that will help this month's sales goals. It will only take five minutes of your time." You are communicating a positive mental attitude, and you are relaying to your upline your *next* level of achievement. Business is a competitive field, and minor differences in the way people speak can separate winners from losers.

QUIT BUTTING ME

When I was a kid growing up in Union Ridge, I had some goats that would butt me with their heads. Today, I have some agents that butt me. They say, "Andy, I will do all you say, but…" This butts me more than the goats did. You cannot say "but this" or "but that." You cannot commit to only part of the eight-step process. You have to do ALL eight steps.

One more thing I would like to say about people looking negatively at their circumstances is that circumstances are relative. Here in the United States, even poor people have it good compared to people elsewhere and compared to people in past years. You think you have it bad because you live in a small apartment, a trailer, or government housing. So many people in this country live in better circumstances, in elegant condominiums, or comfortable homes. Yet, even in your "bad" circumstances, you likely have a refrigerator full of food, carpeting on the floor and a thermostat set at 71 degrees in the wintertime. You likely have air conditioning to keep you comfortable in the summer. I know there are truly poor people, homeless people, in our country, but if you are reading this you are not destitute. You are not like so many people in developing countries who truly have nothing. You are blessed. You may be so blessed that you do not try to improve your situation.

I hear you, but I hear you butting me.

The way to success is often through failure, and in this country there is too much interference with failure. You do not really have to succeed if you do not desire it. You rarely have to step up and try harder in this country, although the recent poor economic times have made many more people aware of what true failure might look like. There are probably more people today who are motivated to put economic jeopardy behind them than just a few years ago.

HELP IS AT HAND

If you are among those looking for real economic security by running your own business, but you do not quite know how to proceed, remember this: you never have to succeed entirely on your own. You have to take on the responsibility to succeed, and you have to take the initiative, but you do not have to do everything by yourself.

I look at people who are learning new things to succeed in business as children trying to do something they do not have the strength to do. Think of a little kid trying to open a jar of peanut butter. He cannot because the lid is on too tight, and his little hands just will not make it budge. What does he do? He asks an adult to open it for him. It is not his fault he cannot do it, and he does not have to go without the peanut butter just because he is not strong enough to open the jar.

Never be afraid to ask for help. You should not be afraid of the way a more experienced person might handle your problem, what he might say to your client, for instance. If you have picked an experienced mentor, he is going to know better than you what to do. What he knows is something you have to learn. Let him show you how it is done. Remember what I referred to earlier about being teachable? A lot of being teachable is just being positive. Asking for help and learning from others can be the most positive thing you can do. So be positive and be teachable. Put your ego aside. Never give up on something you want by saying it is not worth it just because you do not know how to get it.

I always say that there are three things that are the hardest to do. It is hard to climb a fence that leans toward you; it is hard to kiss a girl who is leaning away from you; and it is hard to help somebody who does not want to be helped. You can have all the help in the world if you will just let people know you want and need to be helped. I know because I have been helping people in this business for a lot of years. That is, I have been helping the people who want to be helped.

TIMING IS EVERYTHING

One last peanut butter analogy. In business, timing is everything. To prove this point, I will give a 25-minute talk on making a peanut butter and jelly sandwich. In my story, I start out making the sandwich by taking out two slices of bread and laying them on a plate. Then, the next day, I come back into the kitchen and put the peanut butter on the bread.

People say, "What?"

"That's right," I claim, "that's how you make a peanut butter sandwich, you put the peanut butter right on the bread."

They say, "Yeah, but the next day?"

"Well, just wait till the next part. The next part is I wait another day to spread the jelly. Then I put the two halves together and I have a peanut butter and jelly sandwich."

I prove that I know how to make a PB&J and I also illustrate to the audience the importance of timing, because if you made a PB&J over 48 hours, the sandwich would be a disaster. Timing is important in the simplest food preparation, and timing is important in sales.

Timing, knowing what to say, when to say it, and when to pause and let the other person speak, ties back into association, which ties back into reading, listening to audio files, and going to meetings. Most of all, it relates back to being teachable, working, and having and communicating with a positive mental attitude.

A Case In Point

Being positive means getting excited about the mundane, the everyday, the ordinary. For instance, I heard a story from a guy named Lee Brower. In this story, a guy calls Lee and tells him: "Hey, Lee, I have a positive story, and not only did I capture it, I want to share it. I want to tell my friend about it. Yesterday, Lee, I shook the hand of my newborn grandson, and I am the first person to ever shake this new person's hand. Isn't that awesome?"

Lee asked him how it made him feel.

"It made me love my daughter all the more. It made me appreciate life. It made me think about all the possibilities in this little baby's life."

Then Lee asked him what he was going to do with this wonderful positive.

"I will tell you what I am going to do. I am going to be the first guy to shake this kid's hand on his birthday every year of his life. Then, I am going to tell him how much he means to me on every birthday."

Lee asked him, "Is that practical, and won't he likely outlive you?"

"I will tell you how I am going to do it. I am going to write him a letter as soon as I hang up this phone and just tell him, right now, how much shaking his hand meant to me. When he gets bigger he can appreciate that moment between us. Then, I am going to tell him that every birthday I will attempt to be the first person to shake his hand, and that when I am not there, when he shakes hands with someone else, I want him to look that person in the eye and tell them, 'My granddaddy was the first person to ever shake my hand.' I'm going to start that tradition with this boy."

Do you see the energy in all of that? Do you see how the positive carried through to a second step and how it can carry down the line? All off a handshake with a little baby!

Maybe you have had setbacks in life. Maybe you have lost money. Maybe you have lost something permanent, like your eyesight. Do you dwell on that? I tell you what: in the light of recognizing the positive in an experience like the one in this story, you can overcome blindness. You can overcome all of life's challenges. As long as you do not wake up smelling the dirt over your face, you can overcome anything with a positive attitude. If you will project that attitude, and take it to the next step, you can change the world.

Successful people form positive relationships with the people around them. It is that way even in the animal kingdom. One monkey alone in a cage is more scared than two monkeys together. Similarly, individuals who establish rapport with others and make a connection with other human beings are more secure and less frightened than those who operate alone. They develop an attitude of teamwork and motivation.

Performing ALL eight steps forms a winning attitude in a team network. It requires your commitment, but it also involves the people around you. It requires the power of association. Keep reading. Turn the page. There is more to know, and it is very good news!

Haleigh's Winning Artwork

Mark & Michelle Womack

Gerald Brubaker Bill Lampe

Dame Pearlette Louisy Primary School

Andy & Jane

CONCLUSION

S omeone recently asked me what it is like to be as successful as I am now. The question does not embarrass me. I am here to teach success and to help others attain it, and I am all about achieving. I told him if I could enable others to feel the excitement and energy I feel every day, I would not have to teach the eight steps any more. Anybody who knew the feeling would do everything necessary to obtain success.

If you could have seen the look on my son's face when I presented him with our tickets to the NHL All-Star game in Montreal, or when we walked out into Dale Arena and my son found himself surrounded by all the superstars of the National Hockey League, you would have known how it felt to have the heart warming feeling of sending my wife and daughter to see Carrie Underwood perform in the Atlantis Resort and tell them to have a great time. That is just an example of what I can do now that I could not do before, an example of what making the kind of income that I have made with National Agents Alliance® has meant in my life.

It has been a short eight years since my partners, Philip Hudgins, Barry Clarkson and I began National Agents Alliance® in the basement of my house. During that time, I have continually used my *The 8 Steps to Success* to grow our company and to promote the success of countless agents. Many have become more successful than they ever dreamed possible.

Now that you have read through the steps, I urge you to practice every one of them. They truly work. Look into NAA® if you have not yet. If you are truly serious about changing your life and your family's life for the better, join us, work the steps daily, and get ready for a feeling that you cannot even comprehend until you experience it.

THE REAL RESULTS

What does bringing in a big paycheck represent? Is it just money, or is it money that can now be used to support the local school system, or to give people who need transportation for their village in Africa a way to get around?

Sometimes I look around at the world with all its troubles, and I realize that success has meant being able to look beyond myself and actually see the need out there, and to be able to do something about it. I cannot solve the world's problems, but I can make a small, significant difference. Frankly, the more income I have, the bigger difference I can make. We can all make some kind of difference, of course, but when you are struggling to survive, when you are spending 80 hours a week just to make enough to pay the bills, you cannot always see beyond yourself. When you rise above that level, once you can float safely above the survival waterline, you can see where you can actually do some "real good" in the world. You can follow through by using your checkbook.

Then, to see the results! I cannot describe the feeling I had recently when I walked down a hallway in a local international ministry office and saw a picture of a four-wheeler over in Africa, loaded down with the people who use it every day to make life easier in their village. That same four-wheeler used to run around in my back yard before I made it available for a better use. Now, I am hearing about how these big briars they have over there are ruining the tires on it, so now I am supplying new tires when they need them. It is exciting to know that when my church or some other organization is meeting a need somewhere, that we are able to step in with a donation that enhances the project, whatever it may be.

So, my success means making a difference with my kids, with my family, with my friends, and with people who need help. It means that I can make a difference in a country where I have never been. I cannot do it all, but I can do so much more than if I were just comfortable in my finances.

I feel like the kid in the story, walking down the beach after a storm has stranded all these starfish. He is picking up every starfish he finds and throwing it back into the ocean. The old man with him says, "Son, you can't help them all."

The kid replies, "I know it…but for the one starfish I throw back in the ocean, it makes a world of difference in his life." The feeling is so good that sometimes it builds up to the point where I think I could go a week without sleeping, just out of love and excitement and caring for people I know, and those I do not know, but am able to help.

Keep a Healthy Paranoia

I do not ever want to go back to the way it was before. I keep a healthy fear of going back, and that healthy fear keeps me going forward. I call it my healthy paranoia. I wake up every day glad to be alive and thankful for all I have, for all I can do, but I am like a gazelle waking up somewhere on the Serengeti. He wakes up every morning to the beauty around him and all he has to do is enjoy life. However, he never forgets that the lions are out there. If he loses his healthy paranoia, he is a dead gazelle. I never want to go back to where I was, so I never forget that the lions are always out there.

If you, if anyone, can just lift yourself up enough to be scared of going back, you will see a whole new meaning in *The 8 Steps to Success*. You will stay awake a little longer, read a little more, and work a little harder to keep that feeling, to make sure you are always moving forward.

Too many people have the view, that by focusing to create wealth and lifestyle, you risk becoming a workaholic and you will be the kind of obsessed person who neglects his or her family and turns ugly inside. So why, for me, does achieving success look like energy and excitement and being able to care about the important things in life, instead of just worrying about making more money all the time?

First of all, I do not give in to people who make judgments

about people they call "workaholics." What makes these same people cheer success on the football field and in the golf tournament and not cheer success in business? Is a man a workaholic because he directs his energy, six days a week, to making a phenomenal income when he is able to take his family on a fabulous vacation? Does working smart and being a financial success make you worse than a person who works week in and week out at a mundane job to keep his head above water, and then spends the rest of his time watching TV? How come the guy who goes to bed at night reading to get ahead is a workaholic and the guy who sits in his La-Z-Boy isn't a "comfort-zone-aholic?" I guess we do call such people "couch potatoes."

I admire the achievers in our society, and I am glad to be one of them. I love seeing others become achievers and witnessing the transformation that happens, how they become more excited and engaged in life than ever before.

It takes work to achieve. I still work hard and probably always will, in one way or another. It is what I do. Why does a guy like Warren Buffett, up in years and amazingly wealthy, not just retire and count his blessings? It is because achieving is what he does. It defines who he is. Achieving puts to use the strengths he has been given.

So I do not acknowledge people who look at high-achievers and put one kind of label or another on them. People who have not been where I have been do not know the feeling that success in a free society brings. They do not know the feeling of being able to write that check to the church that is going to make a difference in other people's lives. In sports, we celebrate wins. We celebrate, jump around and scream after a touchdown or a home run or a game-winning three-pointer. Why shouldn't business success, financial success, cause the same reaction?

You Are What You Love

Also, most importantly, faith is at the core of why I find excitement instead of greed in making a lot of money. I believe that my God is a good God, and I do not think he wants me, or anyone else, to be tormented by wealth. I think that my God wants me to enjoy my successes and to give to others. I think my God wants me to help lift other people up, and I would be doing less than what is expected of me if I were to just sit back and be comfortable.

God has given me the energy to do what I do. He has given me enthusiasm. Remember, the word "enthusiasm" comes from the Greek, meaning "God within."

My friend, John Maxwell says, "The way to success is to find out what you do well, start doing it, and keep doing it." Find something that you love, something you would do for nothing. What you love is real. It is legitimate. What you love is who you are. What you love is what God has designed you for.

So much of my life now is about taking on new experiences because I want to and I am able to. Finances do not control my decisions like they used to. Now, when I make a decision about whether to do something or not, it is the experience I consider and not the money. I am more concerned with the feelings than with the dollar bills. I do things from the heart, without having to wonder whether I can afford to or not.

BALANCE YOUR RIDE

Of course, you have to keep balance in all of this for it to work. Sometimes to get ahead, you have to get out of balance for a little while, but then you always have to bring your life back into balance or you will spin out of control. It is like a race-car driver who has to shift the car's balance when he goes into those left turns, then he has to achieve a different balance in the straight-aways. Then, after the race, once that car is a victory car, he can shift the weight around to a different balance altogether.

In work, you throw balance where it needs to be while you are achieving. Then, you can take your family on a three-week safari to Africa and let them see things most kids never see. Now, that is some crazy balance, being able to spend three weeks on a safari with your wife and kids. If you think spending a lot of money taking your family on a safari is unbalanced, well wouldn't you like to experience some of that?

There are people in my organization who love what they do to the point of making millions. I will tell you about a couple of them.

Alex Fitzgerald is our top producer as I am writing this. Alex is a success because he found what he loved and stuck with it. He also had some luck along the way. Alex had the good fortune, after his father died unexpectedly, to find out he was going to have to put himself through college.

That is luck?

Remember, success is built on obstacles.

After getting himself through college, Alex moved to Dallas, Texas, where he could associate with successful people. When I first met Alex, he had just joined our organization and was living in an apartment in Dallas. When I visited him there I told him to move because I was not coming there anymore. I told him I was afraid for my life in that place. When it rained, the parking lot flooded so bad you could not get out of your car. The place had dirt paths instead of sidewalks. That is the way Alex started out in Dallas.

Alex has followed the eight steps as well as anyone I know. Like I said, he is our top producer. He has saved money, he lives well, drives the car he wants to drive, and he gives phenomenal amounts to charity. He and his wife, Heather, have two young boys. Like all successful people, he reaches plateaus, catches his breath, and then sets new goals. He now has a goal of giving millions in one year to his church!

I mentioned Adam Katz in an earlier chapter. He was a schoolteacher for years and a very intelligent guy, smart academically. Adam had a paradigm shift and raised his sights, financially speaking, with NAA®. He now lives in a million-dollar home on the waterway in Wilmington, North Carolina. His business stretches all over the country. Adam's success provides a lesson in achievement. Adam is well on his way in his journey, and he is a top producer with National Agents Alliance®. He and his wife Beth have three children, and are some of our closest friends.

A few years ago, he hit a rough patch and began worrying about losing everything he had built. He told me, "Whew, it's tough."

I said, "Listen, bud, listen to this. Let's just say we have accomplished all we are going to accomplish. You remember the past five years of your life?"

"Oh, man, it's been awesome!"

"Dude, they cannot take away these years you have had. So, go enjoy another day. Go work your butt off for a few hours, then enjoy some time with your family."

Usually, success is more in the journey rather than in the destination.

SUCCESS IS YOURS

Nobody can take away the years you will spend achieving. If you lose what you have, wake up glad to be breathing. Wake up glad to have the chance to succeed again.

Life is for living, life is for working, and life is for achieving. I would not give anything or trade for the years I have spent developing businesses, and no matter what happens in the future, no one can take away that experience. If I had to sum up what my road to success has been like, I guess I would have to say, I had no idea how hard it would be to get here, but I had no idea how awesome it would be, either.

Now, how about you? Will you do what it takes to be successful? It is not that hard. Just step out with a little faith, take that first step, and I promise, when you get here, you will wonder what took you so long or why you did not start sooner. Of course, by then, it will not matter anymore. The only thing that will matter then will be the memories you have of building your dream, and the experience of sharing your dreams with the people you love.

RESOURCES

- Andy Albright Blog
  - * AndyAlbright.com

- Facebook
  - * facebook.com/AndySAlbright

- Twitter
  - * twitter.com/AndySAlbright

- YouTube
  - * youtube.com/AndySAlbright

- LinkedIn
  - * linkedin.com/in/NAALife

- Instagram
  - * instagram.com/andysalbright#

- Recruiting Site
  - * beyourown-rockstar.com

- Sales Site
  - * NAALife.com

- Meetings Site
  - * NAAHotSpots.com

- Company
  - * National Agents Alliance®
  - * NAALeads.com

- Product Information
  - * NAA Life
  - * NAALife.com

NAA AGENCY MANAGERS

As of July 2013

Shawn Meaike
Preston, CT
Websites: NAAMeaike.com and
NAAMeaikeSales.com

Alex & Heather Fitzgerald
Addison, TX
Websites: NAAFitz.com and
MortgageProtectionFitz.com

Bill & Diane Lampe
Dallas, TX
Websites: CareersAtNAA.com and
ProtectYourFamily.us

Stephen & Hollie Davies
Arden, NC
Websites: NAADavies.com and
PriorityOneMortgageProtection.com

Kyle & Beth Winebrenner
Cabot, AR
Websites: NAAKyle.com and
MortgageProtectionGroup123.com

Adam & Beth Katz
Wilmington, NC
Website: NAAKatz.com

Chris & Cortney Long
Jacksonville, FL
Websites: NAALong.com and
NAALongLife.com

Patrick & Suzanne Connors
Mason, OH
Website: NAAConnors.com

Paul & Tamara Roberts
Lewisville, TX
Website: NAARoberts.com

Mike & Noelle Lewantowicz
Louisville, KY
Website: TristateGroup.org

Matt & Patricia Smith
Coeur d'Alene, ID
Website: SelectChoiceNetworkNAA.com

Michael & Angie Owens
Dayton, OH
Websites: NAAOwens.com and
TheNAAFamily.com

Jim & Karen Glascott
Alta Loma, CA
Websites: NAABusiness.com and
MyMortgageProtector.com

Paul & Natasha McClain
Victorville, CA
Website: NAAMcClain.com

John Wilson
Lewisville, TX
Websites: TheJohnWilsonGroup.com and
TheJohnWilsonGroup.net

Kevin & Nancy Davies
Asheville, NC
Websites: NAAExplode.com and
MortgageProtection-KDavies.com

Aaron & Dana Guetterman
Wake Forest, NC
Websites: Guettermangroup.com and
NAAFamilyProtectionGroup.com

George & Penny Wilson
Little Elm, TX
Websites: NAABuilders.com and
YourFamilyProtected.com

Alex & Ginny Abuyuan
Dayton, OH
Websites: NAAPowerLeads.com and
123PowerLeads.com

Christopher Baldwin
Carlsbad, CA
Websites: NAABaldwin.com and
NAAMortgageProtection.com

Jason Carey
Rancho Cucamonga, CA
Website: NAANextLevel.com

Gerald & Mindy Brubaker
Eaton, OH
Website: ProtectionForTheFamily.com

Robert & Brandy Jones
Englewood, OH
Website: JonesFinancialServices.org

Mark & Michelle Womack
Jacksonville, FL
Websites: WomackMortgageProtection.com and
NAAWomack.com

Jerrod & Jennifer Ewing
Navarre, FL
Websites: SuperiorInsuranceProducts.com and

Mike Killimett
Mabelton, GA
Website: NAAKillimett.com

Bill Martin
Rockford, MI
Website: NAAMartin.com

Mike & Michele Alleman
Seabrook, TX
Websites: AllemanAgency.com and
NAAAlleman.com

Aaron Croft
Polk City, IA
Website: FindYourCareerHere.com

FREE!

SELF-EVALUATION TEST!

Do you have what it takes to make your dreams come true?

"Dreams come a size too big so that we can grow into them." –Josie Bisset

Do you have a dream? Thinking you want to go after it?
What do you do next? Would you like to know if you have
a chance to obtain it?

I have great news for you…Visit <u>AndyAlbright.com</u> to get a free
overview and evaluation to see if you have what it takes!

Take my quick, simple and easy evaluation
and find out today!

The 8 Steps to Success
Multimedia Package

This package includes Andy Albright's first book, "Eight Steps to Success" in 3 different versions: a paperback, an E-book, and an Audio book! It also includes a helpful workbook that will help you achieve your goals and find the success you have always hoped for!

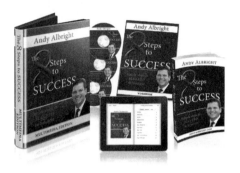

The 8 Steps to Success
Audio Book

Andy Albright's "Eight Steps to Success" is now in audio form! Read by the author himself, you can now listen to "Eight Steps to Success" in your rolling university!

The Albright Challenge

WITH THE ALBRIGHT CHALLENGE, YOU ARE GOING TO CHANGE YOUR MINDSET AND START THINKING LIKE A WINNER BECAUSE YOU ARE JUST THAT!

You have the opportunity to take part in the Albright Challenge, a 90-day program that will raise your expectation levels personally and professionally. My Challenge will change the way you think, show you that better results are possible and help you improve the quality of your life.

Sign up for a free trial of The Albright Challenge today and enjoy:

✓ 3 sample days of The Albright Challenge goal-setting program

✓ 3 days of Andy Albright's motivating email and video series

✓ BONUS! Free online test providing you a personalized and customized skills assessment by one of my professional life coaches - valued at hundreds of dollars!

Sign Up Today at www.AlbrightChallenge.com!

NAActivity™ Tracker